THE
BOOK
ON
DOWNSIZING

What People are Saying

Nothing in life has saddened me more than to see business colleagues as well as close family members drift into retirement without the proper planning or mind-set to enjoy what should be some of the happiest and carefree years of our lives. And the issues all boiled down to the same root cause—failure to live within one's means, and to properly plan. In a word, "Downsize." As an unprecedented number of baby boomers exit the workforce, I can hardly think of any book more relevant to helping more people than *The Book on Downsizing*. This is a must-read for anyone within 10 years of retirement! It is a book that shall save many from the heartaches and stresses I have seen far too many of those dear to me endure.

James Michael Lafferty
CEO The Procter and Gamble Company Philippines (Ret.)
CEO The Coca Cola Bottling Company Nigeria

Timely, topical and hard hitting, *The Book on Downsizing* squarely addresses the issues confronting our generation. Having lived through one of the most prosperous periods in history, Baby Boomers or "Zoomers" are challenged with simplifying and *decluttering* every aspect of their lives and this book provides a clear perspective on rightsizing this "Next Chapter."

Dr. John Gray, PhD
New York Times #1 bestselling author of
Men Are from Mars, Women Are from Venus

THE
BOOK
ON
DOWNSIZING

7 STEPS TO RIGHTSIZE THE REST OF YOUR LIFE

Robert Miller
& Monika Lowry

Visit www.TheBookonDownsizing.com for FREE Resources and to learn more.

DEDICATION

Most significant achievements in life are the result of collaboration and working with others whose talents and insights enable us to create something new and worthwhile. This book is a tribute to the power of personal relationships and is dedicated to the hundreds of couples whose experiences have shaped the messages we have shared with you.

This book is also dedicated to you, our reader, as a resource in helping you and your partner confidently design your "Next Chapter" in life. The techniques and tools that will guide you through the process are revealed in this book that's in your hands. As everything in life is a choice, you are equipped to create your future by *designing the rest of your life*, now!

ACKNOWLEDGMENTS

We are very blessed to have the opportunity of working with our collective family, friends, clients, and peers who have made such a valuable contribution to our life, and our life's work.

Through the insights and life experiences that clients have shared during thousands of personal conversations, we have compiled the collective wisdom of so many and share this with you, our reader.

Special thanks to Raymond Aaron whose leadership and encouragement has made this book a reality. Thanks also to Lori Murphy, Jennifer Le, Jon Hofferman, Kim Leonard and Levi Hoekstra whose guidance and support have made the creation of this book such an incredible experience.

TABLE OF CONTENTS

FOREWORD

What if you could turn back time and change the life you have lived till now! While this may not be possible, we do have the opportunity to change our future and create the lifestyle we want in our "Next Chapter" of life. How? Simply, by planning.

The Book on Downsizing is a guided tour to developing your personalized *Downsizing Plan* by answering the "Who, *What, When, Why, How, and Where*" for that incredible *journey* ahead. *"Designing the Next Chapter of your life"* will be simpler and more enjoyable by utilizing this *Downsizing Planning* process with all of the insights, tools and exercises, including:

a. How Downsizing is a process, not an event
b. Why Downsizing encompasses your lifestyle choices, as well as your home
c. When Downsizing is about "moving on" versus "hanging on"
d. How Downsizing starts with simple planning
e. Who Downsizing is a team sport with
f. How Downsizing can be the most exciting journey of your life
g. Why Downsizing requires your personal action now

Most Baby Boomers or "Zoomers" have been disciplined and careful to set aside a nest egg to fund the lifestyle they envisioned for their post-working years. Others, who have enjoyed the good life, arrive rather unprepared. In either case, many of us are healthy enough to be retired for more years than we actually worked so it is crucial that we "plan ahead".

Prepared or not, many of us have already arrived and "The Book on Downsizing" provides a candid, uplifting perspective to help prepare us for *the best chapter of our life,* those unspent days that lie ahead! While emptying our closets or buying that smaller home may be one of the end results, there's lots of pre-work before we get there and this book walks you through the 7 steps that facilitate the right conclusions for you and your partner.

Successful Baby Boomers themselves, Robert Miller and Monika Lowry bring 5 decades of combined experience helping their clients *"choose the home they'll love to live in."* Drawing on more than 10,000 hours of personal face-to-face interviews with home buyers and sellers, they bring a wealth of experience and a candid, heartfelt perspective.

As both business and life partners, Monika and Robert are early adopters who have been there and "walked the walk" themselves. So whether you find yourself looking at *Downsizing, Rightsizing, or Shifting Gears in mid stream,* this book offers wonderful insights and the tools that will help you and your partner *"design the Next Chapter"* of your life, together........ and live it with passion and purpose.

Raymond Aaron,
New York Times bestselling author of
Chicken Soup for the Canadian Soul,
Chicken Soup for the Parent's Soul,
and *Double Your Income Doing What you Love*

INTRODUCTION

Over the past 100 years, the Western world has seen unprecedented growth and rapid change that has brought much that is good. However, one unfortunate consequence of this phenomenal prosperity is that many of us have become extremely materialistic and have invested great significance in the collection of *Things*. What makes it even worse is that, over time, these *Things* somehow seem to multiply on their own, and we soon find ourselves drowning in a sea of stuff.

Perhaps the most visible manifestation of this explosive expansion is the size of our homes, which have grown to gargantuan proportions along with our prosperity. And it's not just the size of our homes— it's also the number of shiny vehicles in our driveway, the new kitchen with granite counters, the hot tub large enough for a street party, the boat, the two ATVs, the Harley, and the three-car garage to house all our toys.

We, specifically, are the Baby Boomers, the group born between 1946 and 1964, whose unprecedented size has led to its sometimes being characterized as the bulge going through the system that changes the paradigms with each passing decade. And now, as our generation ages, many of us are feeling the need to change our habits of consumption and divest ourselves of many of our acquisitions. But we're also finding that it's not an easy thing to do.

Our parents' generation worked hard, saved diligently, and lived modestly all their life so there would be a nest egg to retire on, and a little extra to be left behind. If we did not live through the Depression and the World War years ourselves, we may have lived it vicariously through the stories our parents and grandparents (many of them new immigrants) told and retold about the travails of losing everything they valued. Through sheer determination, they kept going in those most difficult of times. Though many would say they did not have a plan, their commitment to providing a better life for their children was the single mission that drove most families to survive.

"WE HAVE EXPERIENCED AND PROSPERED FROM MORE RADICAL CHANGE THAN ANY GENERATION BEFORE US."

In contrast, during the past 50 years, Baby Boomers have had a phenomenal ride, a time of great prosperity, including the growth of computing as a tool to radically transform business, communications, and every aspect of our daily lives. We have experienced, accepted, and prospered from more radical change than virtually any generation before us. And many of us have been so preoccupied with getting to this point, we are truly unprepared and have no plan on how or where to go from here.

Hence *The Book on Downsizing*, a simple step-by-step guide to developing your personalized plan and creating the future you want. The main focus will be on finding a home that's right for the next stage in your life. However, before we get to that exciting step, it's important to take some time to explore just what downsizing is and how it fits into planning your future.

1

UNDERSTANDING DOWNSIZING

As you've probably already guessed, downsizing is about more than just emptying closets or buying that smaller retirement home! Downsizing is a life process, one that can considerably ease your passage into the "golden years" that marketers love to talk about.

Downsizing means different things to different people... their house, the size of their property, how much mortgage they are willing and able to carry forward, their personal health, the things (both material and immaterial) they've accumulated—some of which they may not even be aware of.

DOWNSIZING, RIGHTSIZING, AND SHIFTING GEARS

While we'll be talking mostly about downsizing in this book, it's important to distinguish between three related concepts that are sometimes confused:

Downsizing is a process of mid life re-engineering, a time of transition from your job or business and your children to that coveted "next chapter" of life you have long anticipated. Deeply personal, this involves collaboration with your spouse or partner to determine your individual and shared goals, expectations, and priorities. Couples who have already been through this process can provide insight and encouragement to those struggling with this transition and their experiences are shared at: www.TheBookonDownsizing.com.

> "DOWNSIZING IS A COLLABORATIVE PROCESS OF ASSESSING SHARED GOALS, EXPECTATIONS AND PRIORITIES WITH YOUR PARTNER."

Rightsizing looks at our hopes and aspirations. For some, it's realizing their dream of that large country home, a year-round home at the lake, or perhaps the equestrian farm with stables and acres of fenced paddocks. Many people put their aspirations on hold and wait until their career and children's education are completed. Only then do they allow themselves the luxury of considering these things for themselves. If this describes you, then you may be a rightsizer.

Shifting Gears is typically a midlife or pre-retirement strategy. It may be the decision to buy a business, change careers, or step away from a high-profile political or corporate role to devote more time to one's family or health. Whether "shifting gears" is a proactive choice or a response to changes in your personal health, career or business, it's advisable to seek sound advice and ongoing coaching, and to plan carefully in order to ensure success in your new endeavor.

WHY IS DOWNSIZING IMPORTANT?

As we mention repeatedly throughout this book, we believe that it's choice, not chance, that determines everything that happens in our future. It is a choice to accept the responsibility for what happens to us, and respond to life's challenges with courage and commitment. The alternative is choosing to be a victim.

Downsizing our home, our life, and our "stuff" is also a choice. We can be proactive and see it as an opportunity, or play ostrich and put our heads in the sand. Being inquisitive and engaged in life is one of the most refreshing traits in the people around us. It shows they are alive, caring, and willing to move forward. As we age, it's an even more endearing trait.

> "CHOICE, NOT CHANCE, DETERMINES EVERYTHING THAT HAPPENS IN OUR FUTURE."

As Kris Kristofferson said in his hit song *Me and Bobby McGee*, "freedom's just another word for nothing left to lose." Alternatively, for downsizers, freedom's just another word for nothing left to get rid of! However, finding that freedom requires the courage and discipline to "let go."

Like going to a spa, downsizing is a "cleanse" that allows us to do some "spring cleaning" in our life, our home, relationships, and business environment. It is important to stop and assess our achievements and failures, our health and well-being, our financial goals and current status. Only by recognizing where we are starting from can we develop a plan and measure our progress against it.

> "DOWNSIZING IS AN OPPORTUNITY TO REDEFINE OURSELVES AND DETERMINE WHAT REALLY MATTERS TO US GOING FORWARD."

Downsizing can be the positive catalyst that gets us out of a midlife rut. When life becomes too routine, too predictable or mundane, we are at risk of losing our passion—and without passion for what we're doing, we can lose our sense of purpose.

For each of us, life has been a journey full of ups and downs. Each of us has made choices along the way, and it is crucial that we give ourselves permission to bury the "Trilogy of Haves"—*Would Have, Could Have, Should Have*. Sadly, these tools of disappointment, despair, and disillusion can fuel endless recriminations against ourselves and those around us. Developing our downsizing plan focuses us on what's possible, rather than what was or has been.

Like a major birthday or anniversary, downsizing is a reason to pause, to reminisce, to share, to celebrate, and then to move on.

GLASS HALF-FULL OR HALF-EMPTY?

How we view things in our lives is always a choice. We can either see the world through a positive lens or a negative one. While it is important to be realistic, this does not mean that we need to dwell on the negative. Optimism is a powerful tool that can enable us to make the best of what we have and accomplish our goals.

Alternatively, if we allow our perspective to be shaped by the media, the negativity of others, and the fears that grip people as a result of events and circumstances outside their control, then we will tend toward pessimism. While we cannot change the events and circumstances that swirl around us, we can choose how we respond to them.

Every day that we spend living in the past robs our tomorrows of all their possibility. By choosing to take positive action and move ahead, we can create the future that's possible for us.

A very old gentleman we met some years ago left us with a small gift of wisdom gleaned from a life that had been plagued by great adversity. He said, "When the way is unclear and you don't know which way to turn, just put one foot in front of the other and keep doing what you know until the mist clears."

As noted earlier, Baby Boomers have lived through an incredible period, with great opportunities for personal and financial growth. In spite of that, our generation has struggled with the endless pursuit of that thing called happiness. What is it?

> "HAPPINESS IS REALLY A BASKET OF FEELINGS – CONTENTMENT, JOY, PEACE OF MIND, WELLNESS, HOPE, FAITH, AND THANKFULNESS."

One of the gems of wisdom that was shared with us is that happiness is a basket of feelings – contentment, joy, peace of mind, wellness, hope, faith, and thankfulness. Even when the basket isn't full, we can still feel positive about our life by remembering that "there are many who would trade the best day in their life for the worst day of ours!"

How we choose to frame our beliefs will shape our commitment to living abundantly and our ability to appreciate the cleansing that downsizing can truly bring. We have the choice of seeing it as an opportunity to "lighten the load" rather than "losing our stuff!"

One of the great things about aging is our capacity to take ourselves less seriously, and the downsizing process presents a marvellous opportunity to engage in a good-natured competition with our friends. Consider a friendly wager—perhaps just who pays for breakfast at a nearby diner—to see who can lighten their load the most, or first, or most generously, You can create a positive event in the lives of everyone involved, including those who will benefit from your generosity.

Seeing life as a glass half-full can be a powerful antidote to the anxiety, stress, and fear with which the media surround us daily.

WHAT'S ON YOUR "BUCKET LIST?"

In the movie *The Bucket List*, Jack Nicholson and Morgan Freeman portray two terminally ill men who deal with their situation by making a list on a sheet of paper of their "unfulfilled life dreams" and then go off to realize them. We have the opportunity to do that right now in our own lives. But how many people will put it off until they "have time"? As the movie showed, it was when they were almost out of time that the two finally got to it. But we don't have to wait for a crisis, or some undefined moment in the future, to start thinking about our unfulfilled dreams and how we can realize them.

What is your dream for the post-working years?

With your pension secure and the company on seemingly solid ground, your plan may be to walk every day, eat healthy, cut back on the red wine, stop smoking, and savor your time with friends and family.

Maybe it's lazing in your favorite chair, sitting on the porch and enjoying a glass of iced tea on a warm summer day, reading in front of a blazing fireplace on cold wintery afternoons, strolling through the woods with your grandchildren, or simply puttering in the garden and keeping the lawns manicured.

Perhaps it's taking trips to exotic ports of call, spending six months at your Florida condo, tinkering with your vintage 1955 T-Bird, or exploring North America in your shiny new motor home.

Or there you are sailing your 42' sloop to the Caribbean and spending six months each year going from island to island, making endless friends, and rediscovering your mate in totally new ways.

Endless days of golfing, with no one calling from the office, no customers to entertain, and no pressure to be anywhere but home for dinner.

Then there's the semi-annual fishing trips with the guys to open and close the walleye season, not to mention being the camp cook when you get away in October to hunt wild turkeys.

And finally, there's the dream of a totally stress-free retirement where the most important thing is being active and touching people's lives in new and interesting ways.

Whatever your fondest dreams are, it's essential to make them more than a vague wish. Writing them down and telling others about them helps them become real. Make it a project with your spouse or partner, and develop a shared list that allows you both to achieve your greatest unfulfilled dreams. Then prioritize these and, to the extent you are physically and financially able, go for it while you can.

> "MAKE MEMORIES, NOT REGRETS..."

If your resources will only enable you to consider one thing, then take that trip of a lifetime before the life in you runs out and you don't have the health or vitality to enjoy it.

"Pushing life ahead of you until..." was an exercise in self-discipline that ensured that other priorities were taken care of first! Our family, our children's education, providing a nice home always seemed to take precedence. Now that you are empty-nesters, it's your turn to do it together while you still can.

It's best to have memories, not regrets, in the rear-view mirror. Our relationship with a spouse or partner often takes a back seat during the parenting and career years. Reinvesting today in relationship equity is crucial to sharing those unfulfilled "Bucket List" dreams, together. Make memories, not regrets!

DEVELOPING YOUR DOWNSIZING PLAN

When you and your partner are ready to discover all that is available to you in the "next chapter," it's essential to develop a plan to make the best use of the resources you've put in place throughout your working years. A plan gives meaning and purpose to our future. When we proceed without a plan, we run the risk of being adrift, always at the mercy of the next bit of bad news trumpeted by the media.

When we allow ourselves to be dragged from one emotional crisis to another, without a Life Plan to provide a "safe anchorage" or point of reference to help us stay focused, we can lose perspective about our life's direction. This is not to suggest that we should become selfish or insensitive. On the contrary, in keeping faith with our lifestyle plan and the things that fulfill us—including the dreams we have placed on our "Bucket List"—we're more able to give of ourselves in a deep and meaningful way.

> "A PLAN GIVES MEANING AND PURPOSE TO OUR FUTURE."

Whether you're 54 or 67, Baby Boomers need a downsizing plan.

As noted, since World War II, we have enjoyed unprecedented prosperity. With it has come a false sense of security that this prosperity will continue whether we plan for it or not.

In addition, a sense of entitlement has changed our workplace, our peer relationships, our behavior and our personal expectations, as well as the expectations we have instilled in our children (consciously or unconsciously). Even our vocabulary reflects it when we hear someone say "I'm entitled to" or "I deserve to." Many of us will discover too late that, without planning, we may not be entitled to the comfortable retirement that we assumed would be provided for us, somehow.

Whether you hope to start your new chapter at 55, or 65, or even 75, it's to your advantage to start preparing your Downsizing Plan now, before it's thrust upon you by health, circumstances, or someone else's agenda. The more work you do now, the more time you'll have to make adjustments or take action to guarantee a more comfortable retirement.

If, for example, you find that, based on your current lifestyle and projected financial resources, you won't be able to support yourself and your spouse appropriately, you can start reducing your living expenses *today* while you are still in your working years. Consider liquidating "toys" and unnecessary assets that may be consuming cash, or that could generate cash to reinvest, thereby allowing you to retire with enough to sustain a pleasant lifestyle.

Those with more resources—whose retirement plans include large purchases such as a motor home, sailboat, or sunshine condo—may want to consider buying them during their higher income-earning years to avoid dipping into their retirement capital later.

Most importantly, when it comes to having a plan for downsizing your principal residence... do it carefully, do it by choice, and do it once! As this will typically be one of the major enablers in the Downsizing Plan for your life, the timing will be important in order to move ahead with other elements you have put in place.

THE BOOK ON DOWNSIZING QUESTIONNAIRE

As you begin work on your Downsizing Plan, it's very important to stay focused on the expectations, dreams, and responsibilities that are most important to you, as this will help you from becoming overwhelmed.

To facilitate this process, we created a detailed Downsizing Profile questionnaire, which is available at www.TheBookonDownsizing.com, to help guide you on this exciting journey. This questionnaire can be completed online, printed and then saved for future reference in your personal password-protected profile.

> "YOU AND YOUR PARTNER CAN DEVELOP A SHARED VISION OF YOUR NEXT CHAPTER, TOGETHER!"

The questionnaire has been designed to allow you and your partner to complete your respective profiles and to compare them. This will provide the basis for a meaningful dialogue and allow you to develop a shared vision of your "Next Chapter" together.

As you work together on your plan, you can access your profile and modify your responses to reflect the mutually agreed upon decisions of you and your partner.

> "YOUR REAL ESTATE & DOWNSIZING COACH CAN BE AN INVALUABLE RESOURCE IN GUIDING YOU THROUGH THIS PLANNING PROCESS."

If you're working with a Real Estate & Downsizing Coach, you can also print your Downsizing Plan for review and incorporate your coach's feedback in your profile.

Once your Downsizing Plan is completed, you and your partner will be ready to move forward to implement the steps you have identified through this process.

A FINAL INTRODUCTORY NOTE: "LIFE HAPPENS"

In spite of great planning, we are virtually powerless to control events that happen around us. Team discord, health issues, and other emergencies can cause disruptions and require changes to our downsizing plans. Don't take it as a personal failure—go back and reconfirm your priorities, your timing, and your team. Make the necessary changes, regroup and recommit to the process.

Be on guard for the "Deadly Ds" that are always lurking. It is crucial not to let Disappointment, Disillusion, Defeat, or Depression derail your commitment and resolve. In order to move to your "Next Chapter," you have to close this one, and this plan provides the steps to vault you into that new future.

> "NO MATTER HOW CAREFULLY WE HAVE PLANNED, THERE ARE BOUND TO BE UNFORESEEN CIRCUMSTANCES."

Market dynamics have been volatile and can adversely affect our best financial "guesstimates" for our future. No matter how carefully we have planned, there are bound to be unforeseen circumstances to deal with. It's always important to remember that "past performance is no guarantee of future returns."

Health and accidents can sidetrack our plans and projections without warning. Recognizing that the "near future" is more predictable, plan to do the most important items first, so that you and your spouse or partner can experience them together. If travel to exotic destinations is a high priority "Bucket List" item for both of you, plan to go as soon as possible.

> "PLAN TO DO THE MOST IMPORTANT BUCKET LIST ITEMS FIRST, SO THAT YOU AND YOUR SPOUSE OR PARTNER CAN EXPERIENCE THEM, TOGETHER."

Downsize your home and your "stuff" before you have to—it's the best guarantee that you'll be the one to control the outcome and that your "Next Chapter" will be the best one of all.

THE BOOK ON DOWNSIZING

2

LAYING THE GROUNDWORK

When asked how they feel about their future, Baby Boomers' responses range from relaxed to anxious, worried and fearful to ambivalent and unconcerned. The decision of when to downsize is a very personal one, and is typically based on one or more motivating factors. The following discussion of some of these may be helpful in your planning process.

HEALTH

As we age, our health becomes our most valued asset and one that we must prioritize. We have heard repeatedly from older people that "without your health, you have nothing." When we are young with vigor and vitality, we tend to take our health and personal wellness for granted. However, on any inventory of assets, health is the enabler of utilizing and enjoying everything else.

Today's healthcare system seems fixated on disease management versus health and wellness, and often seems to be controlled by the pharmaceutical companies. Frustration with our medical system is causing many people to take charge of their own health.

Internet health and wellness resources, as well as countless books on these topics, are providing a wealth of information at a level that everyone can understand. Investing in our own self-education is crucial if we wish to take control and sustain the quality of life we want. While "anti-aging" products keep us looking younger on the outside, there is a growing urgency to deal with the health of every aspect of our body. One great resource has been Suzanne Somers' series of books featuring leading physicians with breakthrough health solutions.

> "OUR HEALTH IS OUR MOST VALUED ASSET AND ONE THAT WE MUST PRIORITIZE."

Slowly, the new paradigm is filtering down and people are finally getting it! We have always been told that we are what we put in our mouth (or, put another way, "garbage in = pain, disease, and declining quality of life"). The rampant growth of obesity, arthritis, impaired heart health, and other chronic conditions in many cases appears to be directly attributable to the cumulative buildup of toxic substances in our systems as a result of individual lifestyle choices.

We already know the major culprits: Alcohol, cigarettes, saturated fats, and highly processed foods, to name a few, are accelerating the decline in our quality of life and may affect our ability to experience all those items on our "Bucket List."

It is increasingly obvious that we need to be accountable and responsible for our personal health to enjoy a high quality of life going forward. The keys to our health and wellness are diet, mobility, stamina, and fitness. Swimming and walking are two of the best, and most underrated, activities to maintain wellness.

In spite of our best intentions to save diligently and be ready for an active retirement, many Baby Boomers will arrive at the "next chapter" with chronic conditions, old injuries, and disabilities. The delayed complications of an old injury, or progressive midlife ailments such as a heart attack, stroke, or diabetes, can be the "tap on the shoulder" that makes downsizing now a growing priority. Being realistic in assessing our situation allows us to design the rest of life accordingly and to live it to the fullest extent available to us.

RELATIONSHIPS

Next to our health, one of the most valuable assets we have are the relationships in our life. Mankind was not created to be an island; rather, we are born into a family, we grow, we court, we choose an ideal mate and get married, and we have children to love who will love and care for us in our old age.

Our spouse or partner becomes the most important person in our life as we share this incredible journey together. While we are created to live in community—one that consists of children, extended family, friends, acquaintances, and neighbors—it is our mate who is the closest friend we have. We want to be there to care for one another, to grow old together, to comfort one another, and to share the incredible joy of fulfilling our Bucket List experiences, together.

> "OUR SPOUSE OR PARTNER IS THE MOST IMPORTANT PERSON IN THIS INCREDIBLE JOURNEY."

At the same time, we all know if hasn't been smooth and sweet all the way through.

When spouses or partners are passionate about their life and their convictions, they each tend to have insights and opinions that intersect continuously. If we are not intrigued or at least curious in life, there is little to observe, learn, and share with one another on a daily basis. This is the fuel that drives a relationship and kindles the fire of shared dreams and imagination.

> "CURIOSITY IS THE FUEL THAT KINDLES THE FIRE OF SHARED DREAMS AND IMAGINATION."

For those who have been together for 30, 40, 50 or more years, most will admit there's not much magic left. Sadly, the sharp curves and speed bumps of life, along with aging, loss of hormones (in both men and women), and a general lack of regard for our appearance as we age has slowly *"taken the bloom off the rose, one petal at a time."*

The escalating divorce rate of Baby Boomers appears to be rising faster than for other age groups—but why? Perhaps it's because too many of us have just given up on trying anymore. And the dismal success rate of second pairings seems to indicate that the grass may not be all that green in trading up, either.

There is always "stuff" and unreconciled baggage that follows us wherever we go and whoever we try to be with. As a result, *old stuff* meets *new stuff* and, while initially it may be different, it may not be better or easier.

> "THERE'S ALWAYS BAGGAGE THAT FOLLOWS US WHEREVER WE GO AND WHOEVER WE TRY TO BE WITH."

But let's return to a day long ago when you first met one another. There was a spark, and from that spark came a decision to be together.

When we plant flowers in our garden, or a tree in the yard, if we water and nurture them, they grow stronger and faster than if we ignore them and let them fend for themselves. Periodically, we need to prune them back, reshape them, or cut them down to size, but always lovingly. From season to season, their energy varies and sometimes they go to sleep on us, but they never really die.

Relationships too, never really die! Sometimes, however, we fail to lovingly remember that we are in this together. For better or worse, for richer or for poorer... we committed to each other that we would become and remain partners.

And now, well, we are just too tired to work at the relationship anymore and have given up! We know each other so well, what else can there be?

> "SOMETIMES WE FAIL TO LOVINGLY REMEMBER THAT WE ARE IN THIS TOGETHER."

While much is written about the topic of restoring relationships, let's face it... we are all visual people and when our partner ceases to be attractive to us, we may have compassion, but it can be tough to rekindle the warmth and gentleness (let alone passion) that bonds two caring people together.

But before we trundle down the retired lane accepting our platonic selves...

There is another option! As Suzanne Somers and others have revealed, there are doctors and support services that can help us get our hormones back in balance, lose that extra weight, get our muscle tone and mental acuity back, and deal with the heart, joint, and diabetes issues that plague so many of our generation.

In short, if we're prepared to do the necessary work and make the investment, we can keep our relationship fresh and continue to enjoy the emotional and physical joys of being together as we traverse the "Next Chapter" of our lives.

FINANCES

Generally, the first thing most of us consider is whether we will have sufficient assets—investments, savings, pension, etc.—to support a comfortable retirement. If our financial capacity is insufficient to meet our goals, it is important to identify this, recognize it as reality, and start to consider the downsizing options that can help improve the picture.

If, for example, you have been injured in an accident or have a long-term disability that has prevented you from working at your full capacity, this may have significantly reduced your capacity to save and invest. If this appears to be your new reality, it's crucial to "take the bull by the horns" and redesign your future plans accordingly.

"BABY BOOMERS' GREATEST FEAR IS THAT THEY WILL OUTLIVE THEIR SAVINGS!"

As the majority of Baby Boomers have been homeowners, hopefully there is a significant amount of net equity in their property. Although the ideal situation is to be debt-free, many Baby Boomers will enter retirement with a mortgage or lines of credit that need to be paid off when they sell their home or other assets.

Slow to no growth in investments due to current low interest rates, coupled with poor performing asset choices, may require revisiting your portfolio choices. Also, depreciating assets, which includes almost everything except real estate, holds many Baby Boomers hostage. Even those who bought vintage cars or a Harley because they would "appreciate in value" often find they were misled when the time comes to cash them in.

Some of us have invested in a cottage, or perhaps a rental property, with the intent that these will provide incremental capital or an income stream in our retirement. We may also have a property outside of the country which may have significant equity; however foreign tax rules make this somewhat less predictable. Time-share and fractional ownership properties should not be counted as assets due to the difficulty involved in selling these and getting out from under the maintenance agreement to which you're committed.

One of the mantras we often hear from our friends and peers in the corporate world is that they are hoping for the "buyout package" that will allow them to take early retirement, with an attractive "top-up" to their pension and benefits. For those who have not prepared for their future with good financial planning, this is the "silver bullet" they hope will allow them to retire comfortably.

"THERE IS NO SILVER BULLET THAT MAKES UP FOR LACK OF PRUDENT PLANNING FOR YOUR FUTURE!"

However, it is a dangerous presumption to hinge our retirement on the faint hope of an early buyout. Like winning the lottery, the odds are shrinking every day as companies become more financially fragile and lawyers become more aggressive in protecting them from disgruntled employees and shareholders. As the vitality of even large established corporations is less predictable today, so too is the probability of attractive "buyouts" for midlife employees.

If you are presented with this opportunity, and you have done your personal Downsizing Plan, you will be in a position to be pragmatic and act quickly. If the offer is close to what your personal Plan indicates will allow you to move on, then you should go ahead and take it. Experience indicates that the initial package offered is typically the most attractive and follow-up offerings tend to get "skinnier." However, whether you are given this option or not, by having your Downsizing Plan already in place, you can proceed with the confidence that whatever happens, you are ready to respond accordingly.

The security blanket previously enjoyed by employees everywhere is being challenged today. We all need to be proactive and begin planning for change. By accepting personal accountability for our financial future, our personal retirement savings, our health, and our personal safety net, we can live with less anxiety and fear of losing our job.

The death of entitlement and the rebirth of personal accountability and responsibility can only be a good thing for each of us, even if it seems unfair, given the expectations we came to have in the past 50 years.

FAMILY

Many Baby Boomers, whether by culture or by choice, often end up hosting their adult children, their aging parents, or both in their home.

The "Sandwich Generation," as we are affectionately known, often find ourselves being the "home of last resort" for our "boomerang children with children"— i.e., the ones that find themselves in a situation where they "just need to move home *for a short while.*"

On the other side, as our parents age and their health declines, we may also inherit the responsibility of providing them a comfortable last home, which can become a part-time job. Coordinating medical schedules and taxiing them to their myriad of appointments can be very taxing, physically and emotionally.

While we love our parents and children dearly, many couples find themselves having to defer their "Next Chapter" indefinitely to accommodate these long-term residents. At a time when they were planning to downsize, they find themselves in the housing business, often without any financial support from their "guests."

There's no easy answer to this dilemma, and each of us has to make the difficult decision of how best to deal with it. However, while it's outside the scope of this book, it is important to mention the issue of co-dependency, whereby family members—consciously or unconsciously—hold one another back from achieving their dreams. Even if you have worked and saved diligently all your working life and they have not, they feel victimized if you are able to get ahead. Remember that life's a choice, and it is not your responsibility if they chose indulgence over prudence. Give yourself permission to move on!

> "REMEMBER – LIFE IS A CHOICE! GIVE YOURSELF PERMISSION TO LIVE THE LIFE YOU'VE SAVED FOR!"

OTHER IMPORTANT CONSIDERATIONS

Mandatory retirement due to age

Although mandatory retirement rules vary considerably, the Downsizing Plan that you prepare will show you whether you need to continue earning beyond age 65, and how much.

> "PEOPLE WHO CONTINUE WORKING PAST 65 ARE TYPICALLY HEALTHIER AND HAPPIER."

Whether working past age 65 is a choice or a necessity, it is crucial that you plan your finances accordingly. It appears that many of the positions available to those of us over 55 may be less challenging and interesting than we'd hoped, with fewer hours available than we may have liked to work.

As always, though, with a glass half-full perspective, mowing the greens at the Country Club can be seen as fun, and not work at all. After all, it often comes with all the golf you can play, even if it is only at non-peak times.

Loss of Job or Change of Contract

Losing our job is a devastating blow that can quickly wound us financially in the short term, and perhaps longer term, if we do not have a predefined safety net strategy that allows us time to get back to work without touching our retirement resources.

One of the new terms that emerged from the 2008 recession, when financial markets in the U.S. and elsewhere stumbled, was a "trough plan." Simply put, when stock markets are dropping, companies closing or consolidating, and job losses become the greatest fear of working families, both individuals and companies need an "emergency backup" plan to help them get through difficult times.

To address the "when" and "if" of a major downturn, your trough plan should outline several worst-case scenarios and detail how you and your family, as well as your business, can regroup and get through it together.

> "BEING PREPARED GIVES US THE CHOICE AND THE FREEDOM TO LIVE WITHOUT FEAR!"

By helping you to be prepared before the situation occurs, this downsizing exercise will permit you to respond quickly and decisively, if and when it should happen.

Lifelong Learning and Maintaining Contacts

Maintaining our commitment to ongoing education and being a lifelong learner can be invaluable. Studies suggest that today's employees are likely to have three or more careers in their working lifetime, and it's crucial to constantly invest in broadening your career and transferrable skills to maximize your options.

LIFELONG LEARNING KEEPS US IN TOUCH WITH OUR WORLD AND THE PEOPLE IN IT!

Having the experience, the network of contacts, and the ability to continue in the workforce as a consultant has allowed many Baby Boomers to retire on their terms, while enjoying the collaboration and income that comes with remaining active in their industry.

Never stop networking. The adage "it's who you know, not what you know" is more true today than ever. Throughout our life, we all make a personal investment in relationships and have developed quite extensive networks of friends, old acquaintances, and peers (both at home and internationally). Social media have made it especially easy to reconnect and stay connected.

By being committed to continuous self improvement, your confidence and self-esteem will be higher and allow you to bounce back more quickly than others who have not planned for change.

Loss of Your Partner

In spite of the best-laid plans and diligent preparation, life is unpredictable and the untimely loss of your partner can change everything.

At some point in life's journey, we will lose our partner and have to navigate our way through this experience on our own. Family, caring friends and the passage of time allow the pain to fade, leaving good memories to cherish.

"GOING ON ALONE IS MADE EASIER BY KNOWING YOU ARE LIVING THE DREAM FOR BOTH OF YOU!"

While many of us may have been cynical about life insurance salespeople over the years, this is the time we can thank them for nudging us into doing the prudent thing by providing protection for the partner left behind. This ensures that they are able to make the right choices when they are ready to move on.

Our downsizing planning process with our spouse or partner should always include a candid discussion, prior to finalizing our will, about one another's wishes for the partner who is left behind. Discussing this in advance removes all of the uncertainty that can paralyze us with a sense of duty or guilt.

> "YOUR PLANNING PROCESS SHOULD ALWAYS INCLUDE A CANDID DISCUSSION OF YOUR WISHES FOR THE PARTNER WHO IS LEFT BEHIND."

Loving your spouse does not stop with their passing. However, failing to go on with one's life and be all you can be for the duration of your journey here robs your family and the world around you of your loving commitment and inspirational example, and prevents your completing some of those items remaining on your "Bucket List."

Burnout, midlife crisis, or other life-changing events

Bad things can and do happen in good people's lives! It's essential to acknowledge the situation and take action once a problem has been identified.

If we try to ignore the signs and push through, allowing our stubbornness, pride, or fear to get in the way, we risk damaging or destroying what we have accomplished up to this point in our life, in just a few short weeks or months.

When we seem to be struggling, it's important to give ourselves some space and time to find our equilibrium, and resist the urge to make radical changes or sudden decisions. In these circumstances, it's always advisable to seek counsel from a trusted advisor or peers who know us well and whom we trust.

A FINAL WORD

People are attracted to others who are warm, engaging, friendly, articulate, and caring. Our social skills and outlook on life are invaluable assets that can overcome other shortcomings we may have. Some people radiate such positive energy that they become infectious and opportunities come their way.

Circumstances and events in our life can rob us of our self-esteem, self-confidence, drive, and motivation. However, in order to design the rest of the life we want to live, we need to invest in rediscovering ourselves and recovering what was lost.

"INVEST IN REDISCOVERING YOURSELF AND RECOVERING YOUR LOST DREAMS AND ASPIRATIONS."

3

VISUALIZING THE FUTURE

To live the rest of our life with passion and purpose is the most exciting thing we can think of, next to living healthily and pain-free every day for the duration.

Is it possible, many ask? Absolutely, but it's a choice! We must still choose wisely in every aspect of our daily life going forward.

For many people, visualizing what they want for themselves is extremely challenging, either because they've never given it much thought, or because they're not used to giving themselves the freedom to explore their desires without taking others into consideration. Ultimately, of course, if we have a spouse or partner, we will have to adapt our ideal plan to mesh with theirs. However, as a first step, it's very helpful to let ourselves question and dream freely to get in touch with what's most important to us.

> "To LIVE THE REST OF OUR LIFE WITH PASSION AND PURPOSE, WE MUST GIVE OURSELVES THE FREEDOM TO EXPLORE OUR UNFULFILLED DREAMS AND ASPIRATIONS."

As noted, all of this material can be found in condensed form in the comprehensive downsizing questionnaire available at www.TheBookonDownsizing.com.

PLANNING YOUR EXIT STRATEGY

When will you stop working?

If you are not already retired and it is not yet imminent, one of the first things that you will need to determine is a projected retirement date, and what your age will be at that time. This will be important to determine your expected annual retirement income, based on all available sources.

Will you retire completely, or are you motivated to keep working in some capacity?

This is another decision that is key in determining your financial and lifestyle plan. While many Baby Boomers have adamantly vowed that they intend to retire as soon as possible and never work again, for many reasons discussed in this book, these assumptions may need to be revisited.

> "FAILING TO PLAN OUR EXIT STRATEGY ROBS US OF THE FREEDOM TO CHOOSE WHEN, WHY, HOW, AND ON WHOSE TERMS IT HAPPENS."

Is it best for you to downsize prior to retiring or to wait until after to implement your plan?

The timing for this may have a bearing on your personal availability to manage and participate in the process. If you are comfortable with delegation and feel that your team can handle it on your behalf, having it completed before stepping down can allow you and your partner to move on to the "Next Chapter" almost immediately.

What if you're self-employed or a business owner?

Those of us who are self-employed or contract employees seldom have a defined exit strategy. One option is to find a partner who will assume our client base and pay us a declining residual on business with these clients for a defined period of time (e.g., 18 months).

If we have been working on contract and choose to retire prior to our contract termination date, we will need to verify the terms under which early termination may be allowed and if there are associated penalties.

For those of us who own a small business, history has shown that the sales volume of these small enterprises is generally unsustainable once the principal leaves (as most small businesses tend to be based on the principal-client relationship). Since these businesses also tend to have little or no value in undepreciated assets or intellectual property, there is little motivation for an investor or competitor to purchase them.

> "BUSINESS OWNERS WHO ENGAGE A TALENTED BUSINESS BROKER WILL BE BETTER ADVISED AND PREPARED TO SELL THEIR LIFE'S WORK FOR ALL IT IS WORTH."

Whether we choose to close down our business or pass it on to another party, it is important that we get quality legal and tax advice in advance. We need to ensure there is a clear cut-off in terms of any ongoing expenses and tax liability related to our business or practice once we have stepped away from it or closed it down.

Note: If international travel is appealing to you and your partner, another option is to take a contract in another country. Even if you had to pick up the costs of travelling there and perhaps your living expenses, you would have a home base from which to explore the surrounding region. This is an example of an exit strategy that could self-fund some of your "Bucket List" items.

HOW WILL YOU SPEND YOUR TIME?

> "RETIREES WHO TRADE PRODUCTIVE WORK FOR SUNSHINE AND EARLY-BIRD DINNERS ARE LESS HEALTHY THAN THOSE WHO STAY ACTIVE IN THEIR NEXT CHAPTER OF LIFE."

If you haven't thought much about these things before, you may not even know where to start in visualizing the kinds of activities that would make your "Next Chapter" a time of happiness and fulfillment. In this section, we'll explore some general ideas to "prime the pump" and get your imagination going.

Do you want to try a different kind of job?

Working at something we love doing makes our time enjoyable and meaningful, not only to us, but to our family and those around us. Although the usual quip involves becoming a greeter at Wal-Mart or working at Home Depot, finding a part-time job that you can enjoy and where those around you will love working with you is a delightful way to put in a few days every week.

Alternatively, with youth unemployment a growing concern, there may be opportunities to volunteer at a local business helping to provide training for new people, as well as mentoring and coaching them so that they can make the most of their opportunity.

Is consulting right for you?

Consulting means different things to different people. For some, it's a highly specialized role in which one provides expertise for a business or individual. For others, it is simply the opportunity to return to their previous employer on a contract basis to work on specific projects or tasks that may be temporary in nature.

Consultants are also often contracted for projects where the company does not want to involve their employees' time and resources. Depending on the amount of time you want to dedicate to returning to work, this sort of job may be an ideal respite from your travel schedule or a rewarding activity when it's too cold to golf.

Is this the time to take up a new hobby or rediscover an old one?

Baby Boomers were often so involved in our careers that we failed to stop and smell the roses, or develop hobbies, along the way. Aside from more obvious fitness-related activities like golf or tennis, there are an enormous number of engaging possibilities in which to lose yourself:

- For those who love to tinker, restoring that vintage car that has always fascinated you is an ideal hobby.
- Since Harley-Davidson stopped being a "motorcycle" and became a "lifestyle," riding a Harley has become the new thing. Many Baby Boomers are donning their leathers and hitting the open road with visions of *Easy Rider* in their head as they cruise down the highway.

- Woodworking or building a cottage seems to be on the "Bucket List" of many downsizers. Working with your hands can trigger creativity and mental concentration, while providing the opportunity to create something new.
- Gardening or decorating your home are also pastimes in which many women and men can passionately immerse themselves. Good taste, as well as an eye for balance, color and symmetry, has led downsizers of all ages to be invited by others to come and help them redesign their indoor and outdoor spaces.

> "DOING WHAT YOU LOVE AND HAVE A PASSION FOR IS A HEALTHY LIFESTYLE SHIFT FOR THOSE MOVING ON TO THE NEXT CHAPTER."

Are you ready to give back?

Volunteering to help the less fortunate is seen by many as a way to use their time and talents to do the right things for all the right reasons. Whether it involves travel to Third World destinations, working with Habitat for Humanity to build homes for the poor, participating in community service with Meals on Wheels, being a porter at a hospital, or working with a neighborhood youth center to make a difference in the lives of teens, volunteer work enables us to stay socially connected, active, alert, engaged, and involved.

Is it finally time to see the places you've always dreamed of visiting?

As we've mentioned numerous times in this book, one of the passions many of us pushed ahead of us "until we retired" is the joy of travelling and experiencing the world.

Travelling when we were young and more vigorous was great, but now, with our maturity and the perspective we can bring to new experiences, travel can be an even more wonderful aspect of being alive.

Maintaining our vitality is very important if we are to enjoy the travel-related items included on our "Bucket List." Camping in the outback of Australia in our mid-50s with a bus load of 25-year-olds in 113-degree temperatures truly tested our stamina.

We cannot encourage you enough to see those parts of the world that fascinate you and to make travel a part of your "Next Chapter."

Are you longing to be a student again?

"KNOWLEDGE IS THE GREATEST GIFT, ONE THAT WE CAN GIVE AWAY, BUT NEVER DEPLETE, AND SOMETHING THAT CAN NEVER BE TAKEN FROM US."

For some, returning to get that degree we missed out on is a dream worth pursuing. We are told that to stay young, we should remain mentally active—and what better way is there?

Whether you plan to apply your learning when you graduate will be a personal choice, but many find that being a teaching assistant, tutor, or working with children with learning disabilities is extremely fulfilling and emotionally gratifying.

DISCOVERING YOUR VISION

Now it's time to dig below the surface a bit and get in touch with the things that mean the most to you and can bring you the most enjoyment and fulfillment in your "Next Chapter."

What's on your "Bucket List"?

We've been talking a lot about the "Bucket List"—now the time has come to actually create one and lay the foundation for your Downsizing Plan. What things do you want to see and do while you and your partner are young and healthy enough to enjoy them? This relatively simple exercise can have a profound impact by giving meaning and purpose at a time in life when you may be searching for something to interest you. Retirement without hobbies and a plan is like being unemployed without looking for another job. All too soon, you run the risk of becoming ambivalent and despondent, a state that is easier to fall into than return from.

Spend time thinking back to your teen years, your family-raising years, your career phase, and write down all

TO ASSIST YOU IN CREATING YOUR BUCKET LIST, A RESOURCE HAS BEEN PROVIDED AT: THEBOOKONDOWNSIZING.COM.

the things you put on hold "until the right time." Don't be surprised if this takes some time, as we often need to reflect. Sometimes we will find ourselves deep in thought when we are driving, or just before we drop off to sleep. When you get those "aha" moments, try to capture the insights, as they tend to be important and sometimes deep-seated desires that were and perhaps still are really important to you.

> "PREPARATION IS HALF THE FUN. AND, REMEMBER, GOOGLE EARTH LETS YOU VISIT ANYWHERE ON THE PLANET VIA COMPUTER FIRST!"

How much would it cost (approximately) to fulfill each of these "dreams"?

Before you conclude that something is too expensive, remember that we should never underestimate the invisible power of intention and its uncanny ability to make impossible things possible.

What would you give up to experience one or more of these "Bucket List" items?

Perhaps the catalyst for your downsizing process is the realization that you could start that small business you always dreamed of if you let go of some of your other "stuff."

What one shared experience would be the memory of a lifetime if you achieved it together?

Flagging marriages and tired relationships may be starving for a common goal that both partners can be passionate about. Perhaps you really wanted to spend your February honeymoon in Hawaii, but due to lack of funds you settled for Niagara Falls. Maybe Maui and Kauai are just what you need to make the downsizing process urgent, important and worth doing now.

"Successful relationships almost always include at least one shared project they are working on and looking forward to, together."

*What is the most intriguing place in the world that
you've never been to and would love to see?*

"THE HAPPIEST
PEOPLE IN
THEIR NEXT
CHAPTER OF
LIFE ARE SELDOM
AT A LOSS FOR
SOMETHING
INTERESTING
AND INTRIGUING
TO TURN THEIR
ATTENTION TO."

Some people can answer this instantly, while others didn't even allow themselves to muse about the idea because they felt it was too unrealistic. But what if it were possible, and what if selling some of your "stuff" that is not important anymore could go a long way toward making that dream a reality?

*What individual skills or talents would
you like to explore and utilize in the "Next
Chapter" of your life?*

When Baby Boomers are asked this question, the answers are not surprising and range from being a scratch golfer to playing the piano effortlessly. Recognizing the abundance of new research data that points to the importance of staying active, both mentally and physically, learning a new skill, or enhancing an old one, is among the most valuable activities we can pursue.

And finally...

*What person in your past was your greatest
inspiration and how can you best honor the leadership
they provided to you and others?*

Wisdom, patience, and enduring hope are the gifts of aging gracefully. What characteristics do you most admire and how can you make them part of your life?

*How would you like to be remembered and what
can you do to make that a reality?*

One of our greatest desires is to feel that our lives mattered. Many have devoted themselves to the betterment of society and are remembered as great role models and community builders. If you would like to be remembered, this is the opportunity to explore what is truly important to you and to give of yourself, accordingly.

"HOW WOULD
YOU LIKE TO BE
REMEMBERED?"

30

YOU AND YOUR PARTNER

Relationship is one of the most valued assets that we can take with us into our "Next Chapter." In order to ensure that you are ready, it's important that you and your life partner have a shared, compatible vision of what comes next for you both.

It's important to remember that the die is typically cast by the time we reach the downsizing stage, so trying to change the predisposition of partners is usually unproductive. It may be better to focus on discovering some new things you both find interesting and choose to do them together.

Relationships, like a business, require constant reinvestment and recommitment to remain fresh, alive, and content. For those couples who have built a shared history together, this is the richest heritage you can take into your "Golden Years."

> "TOO MUCH TOGETHERNESS, TOO QUICKLY, CAN BE DIFFICULT. TAKE TIME TO REDISCOVER ONE ANOTHER AND CREATE SHARED INTERESTS."

However, planning how to effectively manage your increased time together is crucial. This may be a huge shift in your relationship and may require going back to basics. Re-discovering one another, courting, and finding out who you have become individually and collectively can be intimidating, but also a great deal of fun!

Is pursuing a venture together a shared dream?

For many couples, starting a business together can be a life-changing opportunity. A trendy new franchise, an exclusive boutique, a Bed & Breakfast nestled in a pretty little village by the river—these are exciting possibilities that can rejuvenate you both.

If you enjoy sailing, then perhaps buying that special boat you've looked at so often and sailing around the world together may fulfill a "Bucket List" dream. Bruce and Ann did just that, cruising the Caribbean for a few months each year, visiting destinations inaccessible to most tourists. For them, it was a lifestyle that continually reignited the excitement and anticipation of where to explore this year.

Returning to school to get your Masters degree or finally write your thesis may be a shared desire, a return to a simpler time and a chance for you both to rediscover your passion for learning.

History buffs may choose to apply their passion to restoring a century home, reclaiming the beauty of antique furniture, or rebuilding their nostalgia car. Stan and Bonnie travelled half way across Canada to find a replica 1953 Meteor pillared coupe in an Alberta Auto Wrecker's yard. When Stan had transformed it back into a "thing of beauty," they found themselves "courting" again, in an identical car, giggling and laughing all the way to Orlando for their fiftieth anniversary—now that's special!

> "IF LIFE IS A JOURNEY, THE TRIP IS MUCH MORE FUN WITH SOMEONE WE KNOW AND CARE FOR DEEPLY."

Do you enjoy parallel pursuits (different activities at the same time) or shared experiences?

Some couples are a team while others are solo soul mates who may enjoy being in close proximity, but engaging in separate activities. For example, one partner may be writing their biography while the other paints, or one will enjoy reading the classics while the other is playing the piano.

Some couples join the local country club and enjoy individual activities, then join up to socialize and be together afterwards. Sometimes one partner loves running, and the other cycling or rollerblading, but they are both active, alive, and look forward to their time together. (A patient cyclist or rollerblader can match their pace to the runner, so part of their outing can be a shared experience.)

Frank loves to hunt and fish, while Beth loves to lie on the beach or float in the pool. They create enough personal space to separately pursue their own delights, but never for more than a week or two at any time. By their own admission, "absence does make the heart grow fonder, every time!"

> "AS TOGETHERNESS MEANS DIFFERENT THINGS TO DIFFERENT COUPLES, KNOWING WHAT WORKS FOR YOU BOTH IS KEY TO YOUR NEXT CHAPTER'S SUCCESS."

The key is to spend the necessary time discovering what your personal passions are, agree on how best to fulfill these, and then incorporate them as an integral part of your overall relationship.

Remaining healthy, vibrant, and attractive to one another is key to this marvelous "Next Chapter" of your life together.

If travel is your #1 goal, how much "togetherness"
are you and your partner able to handle?

If your careers have led you both to work outside the home, perhaps you are not ready for being together constantly for more than a few days at a time initially. Like any significant change in lifestyle, it may take some time to work out what's best. Taking it slow and being sensitive to one another's need for aloneness now and then typically makes the process easier and more successful.

What do a 30' motor home, an 800-square-foot
modular home in Florida, and a 1-bedroom condo
on the beach have in common?

The answer is, they can become pretty close quarters unless you are truly in sync with one another and share common interests. If this is not the case, it is usually wise to plan carefully and "practice togetherness" before embarking on that long-term trip or vacation you've been dreaming of.

Spend time thinking about what interests each of you and could keep you occupied for days and weeks. Crossword puzzles and solitaire can wear thin, as does taking sightseeing tours every day, followed by endless window shopping. Doing your homework in advance will ensure that you are equipped to stay engaged and having fun, individually and together.

Veteran travelers will often recommend taking shorter trips initially, as these will be helpful in establishing some travel routines. It is also highly recommended that you practice packing together before you leave. For example, enjoying a European or Australian tour with a new destination every night will be more comfortable and fun if you are able to unpack and pack in minutes. It's tempting to take everything, but after several trips, you'll get into a groove and this process will become much smoother.

Have you typically travelled together in the past?

One suggestion that has worked for others is to start by making a list of all of the shared trips you have ever taken together.

Next, for each trip, list three high points and three disappointments that you experienced. While your recollection of trips taken more than 10 years ago may be less vivid, the data will still be helpful.

"EACH OF YOU HAVE EXPECTATIONS AND PREFERENCES, SO SPEND SOME TIME AGREEING ON THESE BEFORE YOU LEAVE."

Review your findings and discuss the type of trips that were most enjoyable for both of you. Remember, this is a "team" sport and the goal is to individually, and then collectively, develop a profile of your travel compatibility.

Did you tend to travel as a couple, or did you prefer to travel with friends?

This is an important distinction that allows you to categorize trips and determine the potential for success and mutual enjoyment of your upcoming travel plans. Given your past travel experiences together, which destinations on your "Bucket List" would you like to see together as a couple, and which would be more exciting to share with friends?

What was the duration of your longest trip?

Many couples have assumed that if their three-week summer or winter vacations have gone well, then three months together will simply be an extension of the same.

However, three months is a long time, and seasoned travelers talk about how important it is to learn to enjoy your quiet days, when there is little or nothing to keep you occupied. This appears to be a learned art and one that will be unique to the temperament of each couple.

Based on your review of the positive and disappointing aspects of past trips, you should be better equipped to plan how best to enjoy and savor those "quiet" days.

> "TRAVEL CAN BE EXHAUSTING, SO WHERE POSSIBLE, PLAN FOR SOME QUIET DAYS IN YOUR ITINERARY TO REJUVENATE AND BE READY FOR THE NEXT ADVENTURE."

Do you enjoy being self-sufficient or prefer being catered to?

If your partner even jokingly refers to a Holiday Inn as their idea of roughing it, you may not be on the same page in your travel planning. Before including a new motor home or fifth wheel trailer on your "Bucket List," be sure to take some time to find out if this mobile lifestyle is really something both of you will enjoy. By carefully analyzing your expectations and willingness to do the myriad chores that go with setting up and moving your home on a regular basis, you will have a better chance of making a wise choice about whether the mobile lifestyle is for you.

> "RENT THE EXPERIENCE BEFORE RUSHING OUT AND BUYING THAT NEW MOTOR HOME OR VACATION CONDO!"

You should also consider renting a motor home for a season before buying one and trying an extended trip. This will give you a chance to experience the day-to-day reality of life on the road, as well as the opportunity to learn from fellow travelers you will meet in the campgrounds and parks you overnight in. (The RV camp is a unique social environment that some people are more comfortable with than others.) Even if the nomadic lifestyle agrees with you, you may find that the specific motor home you rented isn't quite right, and you may change your mind several times before settling on the right size and type for you.

Do you prefer adventure travel or more passive and relaxing destinations?

"Bucket List" trips that emphasize adventure are often outside the travel experience of those contemplating such excursions. If your idea of a vacation in the past was a two-week Caribbean cruise, then climbing

Mt Kilimanjaro or Machu Picchu in Peru might be more of a challenge than you realize. It's important to work up to these by taking some less strenuous trips first to ensure you are ready and will truly enjoy these rigorous experiences.

"TRAVEL LITERATURE THAT SUGGESTS YOU BE 'MODERATELY FIT' SHOULD BE TAKEN SERIOUSLY IF YOU ARE TO FULLY EXPERIENCE THE ADVENTURE BEING OFFERED."

Even a less physically active trip, such as a cruise to the Galapagos Islands, may involve climbing in and out of a Zodiac or wading ashore on a rocky beach. After researching the various itinerary options available, be careful to match your appetite with your capacity to actively participate for the most fulfilling outcome.

A Final Travel Note

As exciting and enjoyable as travel is, it's always great to get home to our own bed and surroundings again. When developing your future travel schedule, remember to build in recuperation time so that you are always energized and ready to enjoy the next outing. Budgeting sufficient downtime for you and your partner to rest and decompress, both between and during each trip, will help you maximize the positive memories and the experience.

4

NUTS & BOLTS

Having spent some time visualizing your future and defining your priorities and desires, it's now time to get down to the nuts and bolts, and take stock of your assets. The more you know about your financial resources and the value of your possessions, the better you'll be able to create a realistic roadmap for your "Next Chapter."

The first step is to meet with your Financial Advisor to determine where you stand today. You may also choose to seek a second opinion in order to have more information on which to base your decision. It is often said that "poor advice may be worse than no advice," so it is important to choose your sources of financial information wisely!

At this point, you also may want to select a Real Estate & Downsizing Coach, who can not only provide expert guidance and information regarding property (what you own and what you hope to buy), but can help you navigate the emotional roller coaster of the whole downsizing process. (For more information on choosing the Real Estate & Downsizing Coach that's right for you, please see Chapter 7.)

Given the volatility of current market conditions and limited growth due to low interest rates, regularly reviewing your financial plan will ensure your monthly income projections from your portfolio and other investments are still reasonable. These updates will indicate whether your spending expectations continue to be in line with the financial resources available to you. Remember, now more than ever, "past performance is not a guarantee of future results."

> "RIGHTSIZING THE REST OF YOUR LIFE IS A TEAM SPORT IN WHICH YOU AND YOUR PARTNER WORK WITH TRUSTED ADVISORS TO DESIGN A 'NEXT CHAPTER' TAILORED SPECIFICALLY TO YOU."

As always, this is a "team sport" and requires serious discussion and reflection with your spouse or partner. Take your time and consult all of the knowledgeable resources whose input will assist you in evaluating if this is the right time to implement your Downsizing Plan.

Many Baby Boomers who are still in the work-force, but nearing the end of their career, continue to believe that they cannot save enough and have simply given up. If you know someone in this position, let them know that it's never too late to develop a Downsizing Plan, as it will allow them to get a true picture of where they are today and how they can best prepare for their post-working years.

HOW MUCH CAN YOU HOPE TO RECEIVE FROM ALL RESOURCES ON A MONTHLY BASIS?

Retirement Plan

As part of your meeting with your Financial Planner, ask them to provide you with a chart or graph that shows your projected income and what percent of your financial portfolio you can draw annually without eroding your capital investment, in order to ensure that there will be sufficient funds to support you through your anticipated retirement years. As most of our original projections were based on higher interest rates, your income may be considerably less than you had hoped.

With the ongoing volatility of global markets, the anxiety level of retired Baby Boomers and their older cousins is increasing as their shrinking income forecast is forcing them to downsize their expectations. Prudent planning and a regular re-assessment of projected market returns will continue to be important for all potential downsizers, as this will have a significant bearing on the lifestyle that will be available to them over the next decade and beyond.

Federal Pension Plan

In both Canada and the United States, a federally administered pension plan based on contributions during an individual's working years forms a part of the retirement income stream that all of us can look forward to receiving when we are eligible. The details of the two countries' plans differ, of course; however, the principle of providing a safety net for retirees is the same. In calculating the estimated monthly income that we can reasonably anticipate in our "Next Chapter," the amount of federal pension for which you're eligible is important.

> "THE SECRET TO HAPPINESS IN YOUR 'NEXT CHAPTER' IS CHOOSING TO SAVOR EACH DAY YOU ARE GIVEN TOGETHER AND ENJOYING WHAT YOU HAVE!"

In the United States, information regarding Social Security benefits may be found at: www.ssa.gov/pgm/retirement.htm

In Canada, information on the Canada Pension Plan and Old Age Security may be found at: www.servicecanada.gc.ca/eng/isp/cpp/cpp-toc.shtml

Registered Pension Plan and 401k

In both Canada and the United States, the federal government created a tax-deferred savings plan to encourage us to invest in our own retirement during our working years. In many cases, employers also contributed, often on some type of matching basis as a further incentive. The advantage of these plans is that they reduce our income tax liability in our highest-earning years and allow us to draw from them at a lower tax rate in our retirement.

An important part of your planning process is to determine the amount of income you can anticipate withdrawing annually and what your tax rate will be on that amount. This will ensure that there are no unexpected surprises and will let you know how much can be withdrawn without prematurely depleting your plan.

Finally, be sure that you understand when and how much you need to withdraw in order to optimize your future tax liability over the next 20 years. Tax planning is always important, but even more so in the later phase of our working years, in order to reap the benefit of our disciplined investing.

Company Pension

While government employee pensions seem to be among the most secure, recent reductions in government operations and growing government deficits should be viewed as potential indicators that change is possible for everyone. Entitlement, and the safety net that employees have enjoyed and taken for granted for almost 60 years, is now largely gone.

> "GOOD TAX PLANNING IS ONE OF THE BEST INVESTMENTS WE CAN MAKE."

The evolution of contract employment has closed the door on company pensions, job security and an assured future. The glass half-full approach accepts this as the new reality and recognizes that we are now in charge of our future and any investment for our retirement must be driven by us.

Annuities

An annuity is an insurance product that pays a steady stream of income to the investor. The annuity holder makes an upfront investment by purchasing the face value of the annuity with their registered tax-deferred retirement funds. In return, the annuity provider (insurance company) makes regular payments (typically monthly) back to you.

There are two major types of annuity:

• Term-certain (or fixed-term) annuities
• Life annuities

You will need to determine the strategy that is best suited to your Downsizing Plan, your projected annual income requirements, your tolerance for risk in your retirement income flow, and whether you are focused on maximizing how much will go to your estate on your passing.

Personal Savings

Historically low interest rates and easy credit have largely undermined our desire or need for personal savings.

In the past, banks wanted our money in savings accounts, as this provided them with capital to lend to other clients. Their profits were based on the spread in interest rates between what they paid us and what they charged other clients.

However, today's chronically low interest rates and easy credit have accelerated consumer spending on everything from cars, boats and motor homes, to larger homes and cottages; it seems no longer necessary to save for anything.

> "USING YOUR LINE OF CREDIT AS A 'PIGGY BANK' CAN UNDERMINE THE LIFESTYLE AND FINANCIAL WELLNESS OF YOUR NEXT CHAPTER."

Lines of credit have become our reverse savings accounts, where we can borrow from the bank (unsecured) or from ourselves (secured by our home equity) anytime. Alarm bells are finally starting to ring, but for many potential downsizers it may be too late, as they have already spent what they would need to implement their Downsizing Plan.

Your Home

One of the options many downsizers are considering is selling their home and renting an apartment. While this may seem like a viable solution on the surface, it may not work for everybody. To determine if selling your home and renting is a viable downsizing option for you and your partner, talk to your Real Estate & Downsizing Coach. You'll also find a tool to help you make a quick calculation at www.TheBookonDownsizing.com.

Investing in Real Estate

Whether you are in midlife and looking to "shift gears" or downsizing, this is typically not the time to be bold and try to "catch up" by gambling with higher-risk investments. Today's stock market is more like a lottery or casino and bears little resemblance to reasoned business investments based on traditional fundamentals of a company.

Real estate has been and will always be the one acquisition with enduring value, long after the companies and hedge funds, and the people who operate them, are gone. However, as with all other forms of investment, either you need to understand the market very well or you need to have a trusted advisor in whom you have confidence.

The rules of real estate Investment are quite straightforward:

- Buy the right property at the right price
- Take your time and always choose your tenant carefully
- Maintain the property as if you lived there
- Manage your business as if your life depended on it

Your Real Estate & Downsizing Coach can help answer all of your questions about whether this would be a good option for you and, if so, what type of investment makes the most sense.

COLLECTING THE DATA

Now that we have updated our conservative projections of the available annual income stream that we can anticipate, we have an initial "snapshot" of what our "Next Chapter" lifestyle might look like.

"ARMED WITH THE FACTS AND ASSISTED BY A TEAM OF TRUSTED ADVISORS, WE CAN MAKE KNOWLEDGEABLE DECISIONS AND PLAN OUR FUTURE ACCORDINGLY."

Based on this, we have assessed our risk exposure and chosen to be conservative in our choice of investment vehicles. As recommended, this information has been validated with a second opinion from others we trust and, where we deem it to be in *our best interests*, we have modified our initial plan accordingly.

From meeting with our Real Estate & Downsizing Coach, we have determined our equity position in our current home, as well as any other properties we may own (both domestically and internationally).

We have verified the details of our respective pension plans and the ongoing stability of this income stream (subject to any dramatic change in market conditions that could affect our former employer's pension funding).

If we own a business, we have met with our accountant and a realtor experienced in selling businesses to determine our potential equity position, should we choose to sell or wind down our company.

If we have partners or investors in a business we own, we have met with them and, to the extent advisable (by our lawyer and tax accountant), have reviewed our succession options or any pre-negotiated exit strategy options.

Based on the data collected, we have revised our financial plan as needed and can begin to explore our investment opportunities, including meeting with our Real Estate & Downsizing Coach to review the range of real estate Investment options available to us.

It is important to remember that businesses regularly update their financial statements to reflect ongoing changes. Similarly, it is recommended that we revisit this process periodically to update the information on which we base future decisions. To assist you, a Downsizing Asset Summary tool is available at: www.TheBookonDownsizing.com.

Armed with a snapshot of our personal financial status, we are almost ready to embark on the next step of "designing the rest of our life, together."

TAKING INVENTORY

In this exercise, we'll assess everything that we have accumulated to this point in our lives, and determine how important it is to us. The first lament of every downsizer is, "I have so much stuff—I wouldn't know where to start!" Our suggestion is to take inventory as if you were a business. Group your assets in a few simple catego-

"TAKING INVENTORY ALLOWS US TO SEE WHAT WE'VE ACCUMULATED AND TO KEEP ONLY WHAT FITS OUR NEXT CHAPTER'S LIFESTYLE."

ries, and catalogue them individually. Using this methodical approach, you can see exactly what you have and begin to plan accordingly.

To help you with this process, go to www.TheBookonDownsizing.com for more information on creating your Asset Inventory Summary. No matter what you paid for them, with the exception of real estate most items have depreciated significantly, so you need to be realistic and conservative.

APPRECIATING ASSETS

Your principle residence

Start by determining the approximate current market value of your home. Your Real Estate & Downsizing Coach can help with this by preparing a Current Market Assessment (CMA). This will include information for comparable homes that have been sold in your neighborhood, typically within the last 6 to 12 months, as well as a summary of currently available homes that would be your competition if you were to list your home today. Short of "going to market" and presenting your home for sale, this is the best indicator of market value.

From the CMA value, subtract your outstanding mortgage balance and any other loans or lines of credit (that may be secured against your home as collateral) to determine your current net equity.

Alternatively, you can have an appraiser provide a market value. This will typically cost less than $500, depending on the size and complexity of the valuation being generated.

Your cottage or vacation properties

Where possible, have a Current Market Assessment prepared for each of the other properties you own. As these properties may be outside the trading area of your Real Estate & Downsizing Coach, they may be able to contact an associate in that area to provide a CMA value.

If your Coach does not have a contact in that area, you may choose to contact the realtor that helped you buy the property. It is recommended that you clarify that you're not planning to sell at this time, in order not to set up any unrealistic expectations.

Again, you can also contact an appraiser in that area, who, for a fee typically less than $500, will prepare a market appraisal that you can base your decisions on.

Investment properties

Rental properties are also valued based on their market resale value. However, in this case, in addition to the land and building value, it is also important to factor in the net revenue generated (after expenses) by this property. Your Real Estate & Downsizing Coach can help you with this.

Business valuation

If you own a business, this valuation will require the assistance of your accountant, as well as possibly a realtor who specializes in the sale of businesses. Although you may not intend to sell your business today, you should be able to get an approximate valuation that can be used for the purposes of preparing this Asset Summary list.

DEPRECIATING ASSETS

Cars and trucks

As we grow older, we may look back in dismay at the incredible percentage of our lifetime earnings that we invested in shiny new vehicles. Today's low interest rates continue to seduce us to buy expensive cars and trucks because there is virtually no finance charge. However, we still have to make the payments on that shiny $50,000 investment.

We also choose to ignore that most vehicles lose approximately 11% of their value upon leaving the

> "TRYING TO KEEP UP WITH OUR FRIENDS AND THEIR TOYS CAN ERODE OUR ABILITY TO INVEST FOR THE FUTURE."

dealership lot, and another 15%-25% per year thereafter (based on driving 15,000 mi / 24,000 km per year). This is one of the largest sources eroding our ability to retire earlier and richer, so be realistic when assessing the true cost of your vehicle(s) and think about how much meaning they add to your life.

For this exercise, the Blue Book (Canadian Black Book) price will provide a good approximate valuation.

Large boats – sailing yacht or cruiser

Often defined as "a hole in the water into which endless amounts of money can be poured," a boat is a lifestyle choice willingly made by many of us, generation after generation. Although notorious fuel guzzlers, powerboats and cruisers are a recreational option deemed "worth it at any cost" by many who spend their weekends on the water.

Determining the valuation of your large boat typically requires the assistance of a broker experienced in dealing with this type and size of watercraft. Failing that, make your best guess and remember to be conservative. (As we are discussing downsizing, you won't need to be embarrassed by sharing this data with anyone other than your advisors.)

From the current value, subtract any loans or lines of credit that may be secured by this boat.

Motor home or house trailer

Many Baby Boomers and downsizers assume that the major expenses involved in owning a recreational vehicle, whether towed or motorized, are purchase cost, fuel and maintenance. However, according to many RV surveys, depreciation is actually the largest annual expense, with 25% in the first two years, and a further 28% over the next five years. This means that a seven-year-old RV that cost $80,000 is worth approximately $38,000, depending on condition.

For more information on depreciation of RVs, see, for example, www.RV.net.

"RAPIDLY DEPRECIATING ASSETS CAN HAVE A SIGNIFICANT IMPACT ON AVAILABLE RETIREMENT RESOURCES AND OUR FUTURE QUALITY OF LIFE."

Motorcycles

Despite the hype believed by many owners of Harleys and other bikes, the reality is that these are not appreciating assets. To the chagrin of many who find themselves needing to "unload" their almost-new financed motorcycle, the loan against it may be higher than its resale value for quite some time. For a reasonably accurate estimate, try trading your bike in or putting an ad on www.Kijiji.com or www.Craigslist.com.

TOYS AND OTHER EXPENSIVE PURSUITS

Time share and fractional ownership properties

While many believe they are buying real estate that will appreciate in value, their time share or fractional ownership is really a prepaid vacation with an open-ended, escalating annual maintenance fee that you can't get rid of unless you find a willing buyer to take it off your hands. Sellers are often fortunate to realize 10% of their purchase cost, even relatively soon after making their "investment."

Aging properties and less attractive locations may become unsalable, leaving the owner with no way to get out from under the maintenance liability that is literally forever, until you can sell your share.

If you own such a time share, be very conservative in your estimate, as it may actually have a negative value (due to annual maintenance costs) on your Asset Summary.

Snowmobiles, ATVs, Jet Skis

These adult toys have multiplied like rabbits, with many Baby Boomer households having one or more. Few, if anyone, doubt that these are truly depreciating assets. Their market value typically depends on the condition, age, and hours or mileage. Given the high volume of used vehicles that are available, comparable market value can be determined by checking the Internet, RV trader, or dealers. As with other depreciating assets, be conservative when valuing these.

Smaller runabout boats (typically < 20')

This "runabout" category typically includes inboards, outboards, and jet boats. As with other recreational vehicles, these are a depreciating asset and market value is typically determined by locating similar models currently for sale to determine an average asking price. This is an approximate basis for valuing your boat and, again, we recommend being conservative.

CHATTELS

Furniture

The indication is that our disposable society values style over quality, with design trends, current colors, fabrics, and textures being more appealing than more traditional furnishings. Antiques and traditional solid-wood furniture are no longer sought after, as they were 10 years ago. Today, refurnishing one's home every 10 years is quite common, making maple and oak furniture designed to last 100 years less desirable.

> "DOWNSIZERS ARE INCREASINGLY FRUSTRATED WITH TODAY'S DISPOSABLE SOCIETY AND THE APPARENT LACK OF INTEREST IN DURABLE QUALITY FURNITURE AND COLLECTIBLES."

Putting a value on furniture is more difficult to gauge, as it depends on style and color more than age. However, a rule of thumb is that most furniture depreciates fully in 10 years, and fine furniture in 20 years. To determine a value for your furniture, make a list of the major items—grouping such things as a dining room suite, since it would probably be sold that way—and consider what it would bring if you listed it in the "Buy & Sell" magazine, or on Kijiji, e-Bay, or Craigslist.

Appliances

New appliances continue to increase in purchase price and are ever more attractive, colorful and trendy. However, they seem to be significantly less reliable than a few years ago and also depreciate more quickly. Warranties are shorter and servicing costs continue to increase, with most parts being available only as a module (plug and play).

A recommended approach to valuing home appliances is:

Purchase price ÷ life expectancy x number of years left in expected service life = value (e.g., an 8-year-old fridge with a life expectancy of 10 years that cost $1000 is worth approximately $200).

Clothing

Includes all those coats and suits and outfits you hope you will fit into again next year (after your diet)... just in case. It also includes those things in boxes in the attic, the garage loft, the crawl space under the stairs, and that storage unit you rent for $165/month.

The rest of the stuff: What about the many things that you're sure you'll need some day?

Put your books, albums, and other possible "keepsakes" in clear plastic leaf bags, squeeze out as much air as possible, and seal with a twist tie to keep moisture and dust out. Then place them inside a lined cardboard carton or plastic tub. They will keep indefinitely in a cool, dry place. Label each container and create a master list of what is in each one, should you discover you need or want something again.

If you don't miss or go looking for any of the items in these cartons, you probably don't need them. Once you've decided what you are willing to "let go," it gets easier!

Offer items to family, friends and charities in that order, so that no one gets offended. Advise them when you will be making a decision, and ask them to contact you right away if they want anything. Be clear about your intentions and advise them that they will need to remove any items they want by a specific date, as everything remaining after that date will be sold as part of an auction.

What about those inherited "heirlooms"?

Did you inherit your great grandmother's china and her badly tarnished tea service that's still stored in the boxes you received them in?

If they are of no sentimental interest to you, do an inventory of all the pieces and, if possible, photograph each for identification purposes. Then have them valued or appraised (if you believe they are valuable).

"HEIRLOOMS THAT NO ONE IN THE FAMILY VALUES OR WANTS TO OWN IS ONE OF THE MOST EMOTIONAL ISSUES FACING DOWNSIZERS."

Offer them to family members first by sending an email or letter with photos of the items you are planning to dispose of, and specify a date when you will be letting them go. If you receive no responses, then make the same offer to friends and acquaintances with a specified deadline for responding.

Depending on the nature of these items, send a photo of them to the local museum or library, in case they have historical significance. Next, use the Internet and/or papers and magazines to see if they're of interest to antique collectors. And finally, donate them to the charity of your choice.

GETTING THE HELP YOU NEED

Downsizing can be a hard process under the best of circumstances. However, like many challenging tasks, it can be made easier by involving others to get the support you need to realize your goals. Now that you have a complete list of your possessions, the next step is to put together a little team to lighten the load and help make your plan a reality.

For each category of items listed on your Asset Inventory, estimate the amount of time that would reasonably be required to complete this task, and then identify the best qualified resources to help you accomplish it. In some cases, you may be able to delegate an entire task (e.g., arranging for a storage unit, setting up an auction sale, transporting items to Goodwill or another charity of your choice) to someone else.

In the long run, it is always better to deal with your tasks in their prioritized order of importance. While you may feel a desire to get the easier tasks completed first, the more important jobs should have priority.

Choose a "cheerleader" to help ease the emotional turbulence that inevitably accompanies the downsizing process. This should be someone whose opinion you trust and respect, such as a son, daughter, or friend, who can keep the process moving forward. When you get stuck, you can rely on them to help determine what's in your best interest to effectively "let go."

You should also select a "downsizing account-ability partner" to help keep you on track. If the plan you created is truly the vision you are commit-ted to, then allowing them to keep you motivated and focused will ensure that you bring it to fruition.

> "THE DOWNSIZING PROCESS IS A TEAM EVENT THAT OFFERS A GREAT OPPORTUNITY TO RECONNECT WITH FRIENDS AND FAMILY."

Review your downsizing task list with your team and celebrate your progress.

Keep a general tally of what you have successfully "let go." Measur-ing progress helps you and your team to stay motivated and excited. As everyone lives busy lives, those who made a commitment to help you will want to see tangible signs that your plan is moving forward.

Measuring progress of delegated tasks is also important in order to ensure that everyone will be able to fulfill their commitments, and fa-cilitate the progress of the whole team.

From the items that you are giving away, ask each member of your team to pick three that they would like to have personally, and ask them to list these in order of preference. Based on this, try to ensure that they get at least one of their choices. Hold these items back until the project is completed and have a party to celebrate your success and thank the team for their contributions.

Follow up with a short and sincere note of thanks mailed to each team member's home. It is always special to be acknowledged in a per-sonal way like this – many will keep the note and treasure it!

CELEBRATING LIFE A LITTLE BIT EVERY DAY IS CRUCIAL TO YOUR WELLNESS AND HAPPINESS

While downsizing is an important step in our lives, it should not become a career that encompasses months or years of our lives. When this happens, it indicates we have become a "curator of memories" rather than someone who's enabling you and your partner to move on to the "Next Chapter" of your life journey together.

Savoring the memories that we keep uncovering as we are sorting through our treasures can overwhelm us, and we can get frozen in the past. If you start getting stuck, take digital photographs of all your favorite things and create a video "memory lane" that you can take with you. Whether on your iPhone or your TV, being able to visit with them whenever you like will make physically parting with them easier.

All items must fit into one of four categories – keep it, store it, give it away, or throw it out.

When all else fails, simply rent a large storage unit, put everything you cannot part with there, and keep paying the monthly rental until your attachment to these things becomes less than the cost of keeping them. And, no, storing them in your son's garage should not be an acceptable option.

"MOVING INTO YOUR 'NEXT CHAPTER' HOME UNENCUMBERED BY 'STUFF' GIVES YOU THE FREEDOM TO DESIGN THE REST OF YOUR LIFE."

I think you get the point... the objective is to make a list of everything first to get a sense of what you have acquired and still own. Whether you are downsizing, rightsizing, or shifting gears, the key question is which things on this list should or need to be part of your "Next Chapter." (Even if you do nothing else with this information, putting it in a file for insurance purposes in case of a fire or a flood will mean it was a very useful exercise.)

5

VISUALIZING YOUR NEXT HOME

We've now arrived at the exciting moment when you'll begin the process of choosing where you'll live during your "Next Chapter." If you haven't yet selected a Real Estate & Downsizing Coach, and met with them to determine if you're comfortable working together, now is the time to take this important step. (For more information on choosing the Real Estate & Downsizing Coach that's right for you, please see Chapter 7.)

Once you are confident in your choice of a coach, you'll be able to proactively begin your exploration of what you want in your next home and, ultimately, start looking at properties that are available.

> "WHILE MANY
> COUPLES SAY
> THEY'LL KNOW
> THE RIGHT HOME
> WHEN THEY SEE
> IT, WITHOUT A
> PLAN THE DREAM
> OFTEN GOES
> UNFULFILLED."

WHERE DO YOU WANT TO BE?

Since, as we've often heard, location is everything, let's start by thinking about where you would like to live in your "Next Chapter." Once we have a general idea of your ideal setting, we can move on to the type of home you want.

Same neighborhood, different home

Sometimes we are blissfully happy with our neighborhood, but not our house. There are always a few homes nearby that seem just right, even though we may never have seen inside. But if one ever became available, we tell ourselves, that would be the home to downsize to.

Same town or city where you currently live

For many people, "home" has become the community we live in, if not the specific house or neighborhood. Whether our plan is to downsize or to rightsize, we see ourselves moving within the city or town that we currently call home.

In the country

Living in an urban setting, with all of the sports and recreational venues close at hand, tends to be ideal when we are in our child-rearing years. However, escaping to the peace and serenity of a country setting is the dream of many Baby Boomers, who spend endless weekends touring country property open houses in the hope of finding just the right one that fits their dream and their budget.

Waterfront property

Living by the water can be a wonderfully calm and soothing lifestyle, although the infinite demand seems to outstrip the finite supply of affordable properties as the prices for decent homes have continued to rise. Waiting until a market correction brings these prices down may be longer than most of us have to wait. Only the unabated growth in waterfront property taxes seems to have been able to pry some of these wonderful settings away from the families that may have owned them for generations.

"AFTER THEIR FRENETIC WORKING YEARS, MANY DOWNSIZERS SEEK THE TRANQUILITY OF THE WOODS, WATERSIDE AND NATURE FOR THEIR 'NEXT CHAPTER.'"

Year-round life at the cottage

What began as a modest cabin when you bought this piece of paradise years ago slowly evolved into a lovely cottage, and finally what could be a pretty elegant year-round home. When asked where they plan to retire, cottagers will almost invariably say "right here!"

Yet, after spending several winters in the relative isolation of the offseason, many of these retirees find these months longer and more tedious than they had expected. Although the pristine silence is interrupted only by the snowmobiles, ATVs, and the wind in the pines, with relatively few neighbors to visit, it can be too quiet.

Seasonal property in the sun

There's just something about aging that doesn't mix well with cold, damp winter weather. Even if it is a "dry cold," it can still feel uncomfortable as we get older. The flight to warmer destinations has been growing for more than 50 years and has now exploded with the graying Baby Boomers.

Ongoing changes to out-of-country health insurance plans and shrinking retirement portfolios are making this dream less achievable for many than it was 10 years ago. However, even if we can't manage three or four months, we still try to fit in three-to-six weeks just to get away for a break.

Quieter street or cul-de-sac

Noise and congestion seem to increase as urban life speeds up and our community keeps growing larger. The longing to be on a quiet cul-de-sac or crescent where only local traffic passes our home can seem very appealing. Yet, depending on your circumstances, you may find that these streets are also the #1 choice of young families with smaller children.

If living in a neighborhood with other downsizers and Boomers like ourselves is one of your criteria, then you will want to determine who lives around that ideal home nestled in a serene cul-de-sac setting. Before you rush out to put in an offer, consider parking on the street at

5:00 pm or 7:30 am to see who comes and goes. Feel free to knock on the door of homes on the street and chat with the owners. They will be glad to tell you about their neighborhood and the street so you can determine if this would be a good fit for your lifestyle expectations.

Intergenerational home

One of the common themes among many Baby Boomer couples today is the desire to downsize and share a home with one of their children or extended family. They see this as an ideal opportunity to share expenses and be close to the grandchildren they love so much. This can be an ideal solution, where the parents have their own discrete living space, perhaps an apartment downstairs or in the loft above the garage. Should they decide to be away for the winter, they can just pack up and go, knowing that everything is looked after.

> "WITH CAREFUL PLANNING AND LEGAL ADVICE, AN INTERGENERATIONAL HOME CAN BE AN IDEAL LIFESTYLE CHOICE FOR AN EXTENDED FAMILY."

This interesting "Next Chapter" option is covered in greater detail at www.TheBookonDownsizing.com.

Adult lifestyle community

This great community lifestyle allows seniors to live in and own their home, to socialize with their peers, and to enjoy amenities geared to their mobility and interests in a safe, friendly, and mutually supportive environment. Most, though not all, adult lifestyle communities are land lease-based, and equity growth in the value of these homes will tend to be less rewarding than it would be for a freehold or condominium property. One of the attractive features of this lifestyle choice is the opportunity for downsizers to more affordably own two seasonal residences, thereby allowing them to enjoy the best weather, all year round.

We recommend thoughtful financial planning, and a discussion of optimal financing, before becoming emotionally engaged in a decision to buy one or more of these properties. Consult with your Downsizing

& Real Estate Coach to review the market for these homes, and ask them to advise you on the market value growth over the past several years for homes of this type in a land-lease community in your area.

Downtown condo lifestyle

After a life of suburbia or country living, some downsizers are attracted to an urban condo as their primary residence in the "Next Chapter." Others may choose to purchase a smaller unit, such as a studio apartment, that gives them a "place" in the heart of the city where they can go for a change of pace.

Due to the cost of land, and associated increases in maintenance costs, the size of these apartments continues to get smaller. Many units, for example in downtown Toronto's Theatre District, have no available parking and bicycle lockers are extra. Preference is almost always to be within walking distance of major attractions, restaurants, theaters and shopping, yet have 24/7 public transit literally at the door. New options such as "ZIP Cars" provide small rental vehicles *on demand* and these can be picked up from a dedicated parking spot near your condo – just call ahead for an access code, charge it to your credit card, and go!

> "LIFESTYLE OPTIONS IN THE 'NEXT CHAPTER' ARE LIMITED ONLY BY YOUR HEALTH, VITALITY, AND DESIRE TO EXPLORE THE POSSIBILITIES."

If you're interested in international travel, owning a downtown condo also provides an excellent opportunity to arrange home exchanges, in which people visiting your city stay in your home and you stay in theirs. Alternatively, there's the potential for short-term rental income whenever you're not staying there.

THE HOME OF YOUR DREAMS

We're now ready to start exploring the particulars of your ideal downsized home. Although most of us would say we live in a nice house now, many would also confide that it wasn't exactly what we wanted when we purchased it. At the time, it "fit our budget" or "it was close to the right schools," or perhaps that "it was near work so we only needed one car."

Every weekend, across the country, open houses are inundated with graying Baby Boomers looking for that "perfect home." When asked to describe it, many simply say, "I'll know it when I see it!" Sadly, for many of these people, the dream goes unfulfilled because they don't have a plan and really don't know what they want. And even if and when they find it, they can suddenly realize that it's not affordable.

By creating your Downsizer Profile, you can ensure that you find the right home, with all those features that really matter at this point in your life. While you may always have wanted that huge dining room, should it define the house for the "Next Chapter" of your life?

10 THINGS YOU MUST HAVE

Having taken inventory and made a list of everything you own, the next step is to identify the 10 items that are most dear to you and must be in your downsized home. These 10 things typically fall into 3 categories – furniture, appliances, and small items.

> "LIMITING THE 'MUST HAVES' YOU BRING TO YOUR NEW HOME ALLOWS GREATER FREEDOM TO CREATE THE LIFESTYLE ENVIRONMENT YOU'VE ALWAYS DREAMED OF."

Furniture

Which pieces are absolutely non-negotiable and must go with you? Large pieces will have a greater impact when you shrink the size and number of personal living spaces in your next home.

Appliances

Existing kitchen and laundry appliances are often included in the sale of your home. Depending on how long you have been there, your appliances may be far from new and significantly depreciated already. If you love a particular item, such as your stove, by all means take it with you—but be sure that the color and style will match the decor that you want in that next home.

Small items

Knickknacks and curios are part of the memories we accumulate as we travel through life. However, keeping all of them significantly increases the amount of storage you'll require. If possible, consider a "digital alternative": take a photo or video of each item in its present environment and create a DVD, or use another medium, so that you can have them with you and look at them whenever you like. One creative idea is to make them into a screen saver for your computer. *It seems that the older we get, the more we treasure these memories.*

ENVISION A DAY IN YOUR NEW HOME

By imagining a complete day in your new home and experiencing your daily routine in new surroundings, you can begin to clarify what's important to you and take the first step in making your dream a reality.

If you have trouble with the concept of visualizing, you can cut out pictures from magazines or new home brochures, or print images you've seen online. Collect these in a scrapbook and, as you flip through them, a picture will begin to form of the type of environment that resonates with you.

Get a notebook that can serve as your "Home Journal." Start a page entitled "My new home feels like..." and then describe the feeling as you walk in through the front door.

> "YOUR JOURNAL CAN BE A MAGICAL TOOL IN SHAPING THE VISION OF YOUR NEXT CHAPTER HOME, ONE CREATIVE THOUGHT AT A TIME."

What do you see around you? Does it feel spacious and open, or intimate and cozy? Does it feel serene and peaceful, or is it full of light with lots of windows? Are there hardwood floors or broadloom? Is there a family room and, if so, what is it like (e.g., does it have a fireplace)?

Envision yourself wandering through each room, and make notes as you go.

Now, on a separate page in your journal, walk through and describe how your current home feels, room by room. Be sure to note what you love about each room, as well as what you would change if you could.

By going through this room-by-room process, you will be able to identify how many rooms you actually need and will be prepared to clean. You will also become more motivated to "let go" of those things that don't appear in your vision of the future.

Bringing your rooms to life

Using your mental picture, or the photos you found, you can now begin to furnish your rooms. First, we'll place each of those 10 "must keep" items into its respective room in your new home.

> "YOUR DOWNSIZING PLAN AND ENVISIONED NEXT HOME WILL ASSIST YOUR REAL ESTATE & DOWNSIZING COACH TO MATCH NEIGHBORHOODS AND AVAILABLE HOMES WITH YOUR CRITERIA."

Using a piece of graph paper, draw each furniture piece to scale, label it, and cut it out. Then, draw each of the other items you plan to place in your rooms and cut them out as well.

Next, on another piece of graph paper, place each of these furniture "cut-outs" to determine how large the room needs to be to accommodate them.

Go through your downsized home, room-by-room, completing this process for each room and documenting the ideal room measurements. This will provide your first concrete information on how large your next home needs to be.

After discussing this plan with your partner, you can then ask your Downsizing & Real Estate Coach if homes of this type actually exist in the neighborhood you'd like to downsize to. The feedback you receive from your coach should help you begin to refine your plan.

DETERMINING THE KEY FEATURES OF YOUR DOWNSIZER HOME

Having gotten a general idea of the size of home you want, and after discussing it with your coach, you're now ready to think more specifically about the features and lifestyle options that are most important to you.

*What are the "Top 10" favorite features of past homes
you have lived in, visited, or admired in pictures?*

List each feature, why you like it, and how important it is to you on a scale of 1–5 (with 5 being most useful or important). The following is a partial list to help you get started.

- Spacious entry foyer
- Fireplace – gas or wood-burning
- Hardwood flooring
- Breakfast bar in your kitchen (i.e., extended or raised counter-top with stools)
- Open-concept floor plan with few divider walls (e.g., between the kitchen and family room)
- Inside garage entry door (direct access from garage into the house)
- Walkout basement (grade-level access to backyard)
- Walk-up basement (separate stairs from basement into garage or yard)
- Lookout basement (oversized and above-grade windows)
- Storage area (e.g., garage loft, basement storage room)
- Cold cellar (typically unheated, but ventilated room under front porch)
- Covered front porch
- Deck or patio
- Fenced and gated backyard
- Mature trees
- Landscaping

Prioritize your "Top 10" list, based on the features that are most important for your downsized home, and rewrite it in prioritized order.

Which rooms are most important in your downsized house?

To help you decide which rooms are most essential, give two reasons why each of the key rooms is important to you. The following is a sample list of rooms typically found in a downsizing home; however, feel free to add others if desired.

- Formal living room (parlor)
- Dining room
- Eat-In kitchen (i.e., with room for a table and at least two chairs)
- Breakfast room or nook (typically overlooking yard)
- Family room (typically on the main floor)
- Spacious master bedroom with walk-in closet
- Ensuite bathroom with spa or soaker tub
- Guest room or combined second bedroom-office
- Finished areas in the basement (e.g., games, sitting, computer, home theatre, office, or bedrooms)

"SMALLER, FEWER OR LESS DOESN'T HAVE TO MEAN INFERIOR— HAVE FUN AND 'THINK OUTSIDE THE BOX' TO OPTIMIZE YOUR LIVING SPACES."

Entertaining and hosting

Who will your typical overnight guests be?

- Children
- Grandchildren
- Siblings
- Older relatives
- Friends
- International guests

"SEASONED DOWNSIZERS SAY THAT IF THEY WERE TO DO IT AGAIN, THEY'D DESIGN THEIR HOME FOR THE TWO PEOPLE WHO LIVE THERE 365 DAYS A YEAR."

How often are you likely to do the following types of entertaining yearly?

- Formal dinner parties
- Casual dining & BBQs
- Movie nights
- Holiday gatherings

What rooms in the house will be required most frequently for entertaining and hosting?

- Living room
- Dining room
- Family room
- Breakfast room
- Deck or patio
- Guest room
- Recreation room
- Other

Overnight guests

- How many nights per year would you typically host overnight guests?
- How many guests do you typically host at one time?
- How long do your overnight guests typically stay?
- How many nights per month would you typically host children's sleepovers at your home?

Maintaining your next home

- How many hours per week are you willing to invest personally?
- Will you do your own home maintenance or will you hire a handyperson to do it (e.g., window cleaning, painting, cleaning gutters)?
- Do you currently employ a cleaning person and will you continue to have someone for your next home?

- Do you enjoy cutting grass and doing yard maintenance (e.g., fertilizing, weed control)?
- Where applicable, will you do your own snow removal or contract this task?
- Do you enjoy gardening, trimming, weeding, and getting your hands in the earth, or would you prefer low-maintenance gardens?

Storage space

Having downsized, how much and what kind of storage space do you anticipate needing?

- Closets, basement, garage mezzanine
- Kitchen storage
- Garden shed for yard equipment and tools
- Garage space for vehicles
- Driveway space for vehicles

> "STORAGE SPACE CAN BE A BLESSING AND A CURSE – BE CAREFUL HOW MUCH YOU WISH FOR."

VISUALIZE YOUR SURROUNDINGS

Now that you have a picture of what the inside of your house should look like, let's step outside and look around. Some Baby Boomers are seeking a tranquil and serene lifestyle where they can hear the birds chirping. This may require finding a home in an older established neighborhood where bedrooms are smaller and ensuite bathrooms do not exist. If a large garage to accommodate your vintage car or your woodworking shop is high on the list, you may need to compromise to find the ideal mix of features. Being realistic during this process will assist you and your partner in finding the right balance.

Yard and gardens

Is the yard sunny, shaded, fenced, private, open, or terraced?

Being able to describe these characteristics can be extremely helpful to your Downsizing & Real Estate Coach, as it allows them to zero in on specific neighborhoods and streets. If you require a fenced yard, it's also important to clarify whether it's for privacy or to keep pets and grandchildren in the safety of your yard.

Does it overlook the woods, a park, a field, or other homes?

A key priority for many downsizers is to have no one living behind their next home. With the exception of corner lots, most neighborhood homes are bounded on three sides by other houses, which limits the availability of this degree of privacy. In developing your Downsizing Plan, defining the characteristics that you value most and prioritizing these makes trade-offs easier and minimizes your stress when determining the fit of any property.

Are there gardens that you can maintain and add to?

If gardening is important to you and if, for example, you prefer a south-facing backyard for your future vegetable and flower gardens, communicating this to your Downsizing & Real Estate Coach will be very helpful in minimizing the number of unqualified properties they will present for your consideration.

Are there lawns and bushes to be trimmed regularly?

You have already indicated the ideal amount of maintenance for you. Baby Boomers often describe the ideal yard as big enough to satisfy the gardener in their household and small enough that it doesn't interfere with your golf game. If a property has been painstakingly maintained by the previous owner, be sure that you have the passion and energy to keep it up. Should the house be ideal in every other way, then perhaps a gardener could be contracted, or the gardens could be "downsized."

> "DOWNSIZERS CAN ENJOY A CONDO LIFESTYLE IN ANY 'NEXT CHAPTER' HOME WITH A LOCAL PROPERTY MAINTENANCE PROVIDER THAT CATERS TO HOMEOWNERS."

Are the trees evergreen or do they have leaves that require raking?

One of the chores that can become tedious in mature neighborhoods or wooded country settings is the annual fall cleanup. While leaf blowers and mulchers have made this task less onerous, for several weeks each autumn, there is a perpetual cleanup. Those who love the setting, but not the maintenance, may choose to set all of their service providers up front on annual contracts. In this way, they can enjoy the beauty without the work.

Streetscape (the houses around you)

Although each feature you select is important to the overall experience of living in your "Next Chapter" home, the streetscape is what you will drive past every time you come and go. Over time, this has a profound effect on your enjoyment of the home you have chosen.

Is there a sidewalk in front of your house?

While this was more important when our children were small to ensure that they weren't riding their bicycles in the street, most downsizers with a passion for landscaping and gardens prefer to have an uninterrupted front lawn. Conversely, having people stroll by and admire their gardens is important to some Baby Boomers. If you enjoy chatting with the neighbors and dog walkers passing by, you should tell your coach that this is a positive feature for you.

Is there a tree on the boulevard in front of your house?

This is a nice feature, as tree-lined streets mature to create the serene feeling that you may be seeking. Even in newer neighborhoods, the trees, although smaller, tend to grow quite quickly. Are there trees on your lawn or your neighbor's lawn? Landscaping often adds to the feeling of a neighborhood, and the degree to which the neighboring yards are maintained is often a good indicator of how they care for their homes, as well.

Is the street quiet or is there traffic going past regularly?

One characteristic that is often underrated as we age is the degree of socialization we enjoy. Too often, maturing couples find themselves isolated in a neighborhood with few visitors, or even people passing by. Front-porch living is often seen as highly desirable among downsizers, so much so that developers and urban planners have begun to create new "urbanation" neighborhoods, where the lots are wider and not as deep. Garages are located beside the house, which allows for a roomy front porch and lots of light through larger front windows.

> "AS WE AGE, THE OPPORTUNITY TO SOCIALIZE AND BE AMONG FRIENDLY PEOPLE BECOMES INCREASINGLY IMPORTANT."

However you feel about the amount of traffic on the street, it's a good thing to communicate to your Real Estate & Downsizing Coach, as this too will help to identify those neighborhoods where your ideal home may be located.

What are the type and style of houses nearby?

While some neighborhoods were intended by the developer and builders to have an attractive streetscape, the result often turned out quite different. As home buyers typically had the option of choosing the style of house and which lot they wanted it on, the ideal mix of homes did not always materialize. Some streets may have nothing but large two-story homes, while others include detached and attached homes, bungalows and two-story homes, larger executive and more affordable homes, all nestled within one or two city blocks.

Are they newer or older-style homes?

While the idealistic downsizer wants "an open-concept bungalow with a walk-out basement on a ravine, a large master bedroom with ensuite and walk-in closet, an awesome kitchen, and a two-car garage on a large mature-treed lot in the older part of town," unless an older home was torn down and replaced by a new one, it's unlikely that such a property exists. In developing your Downsizing Plan, you have prioritized the features that will enable you to enjoy your "Next Chapter" home. The importance of the relationship you develop with your Real Estate & Downsizing Coach, and their ability to patiently walk you through this evaluation and trade-off process, cannot be overestimated.

Does your home have a garage and is there a single or double driveway?

One of the criteria for many home buyers, including downsizers, is the ability to park as many cars as possible in their driveway. A sidewalk on the front of your property typically limits a single driveway to one car in the driveway and one in the garage, if there is one. A double or triple driveway will typically hold two or three cars if there is a sidewalk, and perhaps four or six if the sidewalk is on the opposite side of the street.

Some properties on busier streets have a boulevard wide enough to park a second vehicle between the sidewalk and the curb. This is less appealing, but may be an acceptable trade-off with a house that is perfect in every other way. Parking your car crossways on the end of your driveway may be legal, but it can be unattractive when someone pulls up in front of your home. If you find this unappealing, this will rule out certain neighborhoods with smaller driveways and multiple vehicles per household.

Neighborhood

Ideally, it's recommended that you choose the neighborhood first, then the street, and finally the house. The reasoning behind this is that you cannot move the house should you find that you dislike the neighborhood. However, the home can sometimes be modified so that it becomes the right home on the right street.

As you drive around the neighborhood, do you pass many stop signs or traffic lights?

Although this may seem to be a small thing, these traffic modulators will affect your driving experience each time you come and go in your car. A busy intersection without a stoplight, or multiple four-way-stop intersections, can become annoying, as well as more dangerous as we age and tend to become less attentive when driving.

> "Walking helps sustain our health, and proximity to shops, parks, and points of interest is a great inducement to exercise."

Are there stores and shopping nearby?

If you like being able to walk to the store for milk or bread, you should know that this is not a characteristic of many newer neighborhoods. In a society where most households have two or more cars, local variety stores tend not to be within walking distance. Being close to shopping, and services such as pharmacies and physicians, is increasingly important for aging Baby Boomers who choose to stay in their homes longer, even if they're no longer able to drive.

Are there any restaurants close by (within 4–8 blocks)?

This tends to be a convenience factor for those of us who enjoy dining out frequently. While it may not be as healthy, for those who don't enjoy cooking every day, this is important. As we grow older, being able to walk to most of our favorite places is a great convenience, and this tends to be another desirable feature.

Is there a school, a library, a community center, or a place of worship nearby?

Being close to a school is often a mixed blessing. While some downsizers may enjoy having lively little people going by daily, this is not everyone's preference. A public library or community center within walking distance can be a huge bonus, although not a necessity as long as we're driving. However, if this is intended to be our home beyond our personal driving years, public transit access to these facilities will be increasingly important.

Are most of the people you pass on the street about your age, younger, or older?

The average age of residents is an early indicator of a neighborhood's profile and may suggest whether you'll feel comfortable there. Neighborhoods go through cycles, starting with mostly young families—many of whom will stay through their child-rearing years—moving in when they're new. As a result, when a neighborhood is approximately 15 to 17 years old, the older children start going off to college and, within a few years, there are very few children. As these homes begin to turn over and new families with children move in, there are seldom as many children as in a newer neighborhood.

Are people walking or does everyone travel in their cars?

Are there convenient bus stops nearby and, should you not be able to drive, does the public transit system have regular service on routes that pass the amenities that are important to you? Some neighborhoods are conducive to strolling or walking, which is an attractive feature to many downsizers at a time in our lives when exercise is important and walking provides an ideal low-impact outing.

Envisioning Your Other "Seasonal" Homes

Many downsizers are looking to reinvest much of the equity from their principal residence into one or more downsizer homes. The concept of seasonal homes has grown significantly, with retirees having access to more equity from the sale of their family home due to significant price inflation since the early 1970s.

While having a family cottage at the lake has been a growing trend for almost 100 years, the winter home in Florida, Texas, or Arizona has only become prevalent

"WHEN CONSIDERING SEASONAL HOMES, RENTING BEFORE BUYING IS ALWAYS A GOOD IDEA TO HELP MAKE THE RIGHT CHOICE, THE FIRST TIME."

in the past 30 years. Highway coach-sized motor homes have grown increasingly luxurious, and have become yet another type of seasonal residence for affluent retirees who invested carefully or retired from executive positions with lucrative pension plans.

While many of these couples may already have two homes—the summer cottage and the winter home—a third home used as a "permanent home base" is a new trend. This is for the "shoulder seasons," which are defined as six weeks in early spring (i.e., March and part of April) and again in the late fall (November and part of December).

Visualizing the Location of Your Seasonal Home

Summer homes are typically on lakes and major waterways. While boating and water sports provide entertainment and fun when the family is visiting, nothing compares with the tranquility of a quiet evening listening to the loon's call, or the mystique of mist on the lake in the morning.

Most waterfront properties today are year-round homes. As property taxes have soared for this type of property, people have felt the need to enjoy them all year long to rationalize the investment. Winter sports, including ice fishing, cross-country skiing, snowmobiling, and ATVs, are all part of a four-season lifestyle at the cottage today.

Winter homes vary greatly, depending on the lifestyle, age, budget and location preference of individual downsizers. Condo townhomes and apartments are popular winter homes for those looking to minimize off-season maintenance responsibilities. Perhaps, like many Baby Boomers, you may find your niche within one of the countless Adult Lifestyle Communities that dot the countryside today.

Properties on the inland waterways, lakes, or golf courses tend to be somewhat more expensive to purchase, but they may retain their value and be easier to resell later. As with all properties, prices will depend on location, proximity to amenities, and warmer weather in December and January. Florida, Texas, and Arizona have been the primary drive-to destinations. Mexico and many of the Caribbean Islands are home to others.

Whether owned or leased, these winter residences become home for a few weeks to a few months each winter. The ideal seasonal residence style and location for you and your partner can best be determined by completing your Downsizing Profile, which can be found at www.TheBookonDownsizing.com.

6

A BRIEF GUIDE TO PROPERTIES

A home is the relationship between the structure you live in and the life that you live in it. Whether positive or negative, fulfilling or empty, constructive or debilitating, your lifestyle and the house you reside in are closely linked. As seen by others, your home tends to be a reflection of how you and your partner see the world. It can be your cocoon when you are feeling particularly vulnerable, or your oyster when you are bursting to share your happiness and prosperity with friends, family, and others.

Here we provide some terminology to help you navigate the home market.

> "OUR HOME AND OUR CONNECTION TO IT HAVE A PROFOUND IMPACT ON OUR CREATIVITY, OUR RESILIENCE, AND OUR ENDURING PASSION FOR LIFE."

TYPE

There are four basic types of houses to choose from:
- Detached – Not connected to any other house.
- Semi-Detached – Connected to another house by a common living wall.

- Link – Typically, connected to one or more houses at the foundation. Aboveground, they appear to be detached houses. Linking their foundations reduces construction costs while using less land.
- Attached Row House or Townhouse – One of a row of homes connected to two other units by a common living wall or garage wall. The *End Unit* is the last home in a row or townhouse block. It is connected on only one side to another house and provides the features of a semi-detached at the price of a townhouse.

STYLE

There are typically five styles of houses:

Single-Story

Bungalow – Typically fits on narrow lots, 40' or less. May be two or more steps up from ground level to the front door. There are no steps to navigate on the main floor once inside the house. Typically a bungalow has a full flight of 10–12 steps down to the basement level.

> "PERHAPS THE MOST SOUGHT-AFTER DOWNSIZING HOME IS AN OPEN-CONCEPT BUNGALOW OR RANCH-STYLE HOME WITH A BASEMENT AND TWO-CAR GARAGE."

Raised, Split-Entry, or Bi-Level Bungalow – Similar to the bungalow, however the 10–12 steps between floors are split into two staircases—one that goes up from the foyer to the living area and the other that goes down to the basement.

Ranch – This style of home is ideally suited to 60' or wider lots and is generally found in older, executive-home neighborhoods where there are larger lots and wider frontages. The new "wide/shallow-lot" neighborhoods are promoted as a more intimate, urban, "downtown" experience, complete with features like front porches and recessed garages.

Multi-Level

Split-levels were typically built as three-level, four-level, or five-level houses. This style of home was very popular from the early 1960s through the late 1980s, but lost appeal due to their having so many stairs. The actual number of steps in a four-level side-split or back-split house is the same as those going from the second floor to the basement in a two-story, but the latter has become much more popular in the past 20 years.

Side-Split – Although there are several variations within each style of multi-level home, a side-split is a ranch-style home that is built as four offset levels with four sets of stairs, each approximately 4–8 steps.

Back-Split – Like its cousin the bungalow, this style of house was designed to fit on narrower lots of 40' or less. It has a similar staircase configuration to the side-split. This home style was often built on a ravine or terraced lot, as it provided the potential for three above-grade-level walkouts.

Front-Split – These are typically identified by the single- or double-car garage built under the living area of the home. They tended to be built on lots that sloped down from the backyard to the street, and appear to be two-story homes in the front and single-story homes with a grade-level walkout off the main floor from the rear.

Two-Story

This has become the prevalent style in the last 20 years, due in part to its capacity to include more living space on less land than any other style. Two-story homes are also the most common style of attached row houses for the same reason. Depending on the slope of the lot, the home buyer can choose from such options as walkout basements, multi-tier decks, and other creative lifestyle and landscaping variations when having the home built. For downsizers, the number of steps can be a disincentive, depending on their age and mobility.

1½ Story

This relatively simple style of house offers the benefits of a loft-type second story in a bungalow or ranch structure by increasing the pitch or slope of the roof. It became very popular during the building boom for returning veterans after the Second World War, and these are typically found in neighborhoods referred to as "wartime housing."

"NEWER 1½-STORY MODELS WITH A LARGE MAIN FLOOR MASTER, ENSUITE AND LAUNDRY IS AN INCREASINGLY POPULAR FORMAT FOR DOWNSIZER HOMES."

In recent years, this is becoming a favorite format for new downsizer homes that are being built with large main-floor layouts that include a spacious master bedroom with ensuite, laundry, and all the latest amenities. The loft or upper level is typically two guest bedrooms with a bathroom for their convenience.

While many of the original wartime houses still exist, they are less popular with Baby Boomers, as the main floor tends to be comprised of several small rooms, including a master bedroom that feels "more like a closet." The upper rooms in these traditional homes are also tiny and often poorly insulated by today's standards.

2½ Story

These homes may be found in a wide range of neighborhoods, including classic century farm homes from a bygone era dotting the countryside, as well as grand residences in older downtown urban areas. More recently, they have been built to provide incremental living space within the footprint of a traditional two-story home. As with the 1½-story home, by raising the slope or pitch of the roof, the builder was able to create a significant amount of storage or living space, with quaint dormer windows that give unique character to these homes in whatever era they were built.

Determining the Features of the Home That's Ideal for You

Freehold Ownership

Here the owner owns the house and the grounds. Freehold homes offer the most privacy and homeowners are free to decorate and renovate as they please. The owner is also responsible for all the maintenance of the interior and exterior of the house. Freehold is the most common type of home ownership.

Condominium Ownership

The homeowner owns the unit and shares the ownership of common elements. Condos are usually apartment buildings, but can also include townhouse developments or developments of detached buildings on private lanes or roadways. The homeowner is responsible for the interior area of the unit (everything from the plaster in) and the condominium association is responsible for the upkeep of the exterior of the building, the common interior elements (halls, elevators, parking garages) and the grounds.

Condos often have strict rules regarding noise, use of common areas and renovations to a homeowner's individual unit, and residents often enjoy less privacy than residents of freehold homes. On the plus side, condos tend to be less expensive to buy, since they share common elements and are usually smaller. However, all condo owners pay a monthly fee to the association to cover maintenance costs and common (or shared) utility fees.

Why Should Downsizers Consider a Condominium Lifestyle?

The words most often heard from downsizers considering a condominium lifestyle is, "I want to turn the key and go away without worrying about anything." This freedom is invaluable to those who want to focus their time and energy on things outside of maintaining their home. While they may truly enjoy being home and the ambiance they are able to create in their condominium apartment or townhome,

> "ONE SIZE DOES NOT FIT ALL: THERE ARE MANY EXCITING CONDO VARIANTS THAT YOUR REAL ESTATE & DOWNSIZING COACH CAN EXPLORE WITH YOU."

their career, travel, sports, and other hobbies are their priorities. For some Baby Boomers, poor health or other circumstances make it difficult for them to manage the tasks associated with home maintenance. For them, the choice of condominium living is an easy one.

For those who have chosen to downsize, the smaller size of a condo provides encouragement to simplify and "minimalize." The task of fitting their 2200-square-foot, four-bedroom home into an 800-square-foot, two-bedroom condo apartment is typically the catalyst that expedites the process of letting go of "stuff" more quickly.

"Snowbirds" and cottagers also find it much easier to maintain multiple residences when at least one of these is a condominium. Cutting grass and maintaining one property can be a major time investment; trying to keep up with two properties leaves little time to enjoy the other things we want to do.

When should I consider moving to a condominium?

The first indication that it may be time to downsize and "let go" is when maintaining the grounds, tending the gardens, and puttering in the garage are becoming less important and enjoyable. Many Baby Boomers find themselves becoming such avid travelers that they are actually away from home more often than they are there. Even if they have contracted the maintenance and home security to others, eventually the realization that they have multiple destinations they call home for part of the year makes their traditional residence less important.

At this point, many will choose to simplify, and a condominium apartment or townhome can provide the right blend of lifestyle, freedom and ambiance. As they age, more and more Baby Boomers start seriously considering an urban home base, with public transit to healthcare services, shopping and amenities. While they are not ready to give up their lakeside or country property, buying a condo before they need it becomes an increasingly important priority in their overall Downsizing Plan.

WHAT CONDOMINIUM LIFESTYLE IS BEST FOR YOU?

Detached Condominiums

As these units have more property around them, they tend to cost more both in terms of purchase price and the monthly property maintenance. Although they have less common area, the larger grounds can be more expensive to maintain. With these properties, there tends to be limited parking, but also opportunities for keeping gardens to personalize the area around your home.

Attached Condo Townhouses

Condominium townhomes are typically available in two-story or multi-level styles, and infrequently as bungalows. While bungalow townhomes are attractive to a wide range of downsizers, they tend to be limited to communities where land costs allow them to be built more affordably. Townhome condos are generally available in two variations:

> "WITH LAND COSTS ESCALATING, NEW CONDOS ARE OFTEN BUILT WITH MULTIPLE FLOORS AND STAIRS, WHICH CAN BE CHALLENGING AS WE GROW OLDER."

- Smaller affordable townhomes with two or three bedrooms, ranging from 900 to 1300 square feet.
- Larger executive townhomes with more elegant features and up to four bedrooms, ranging from 1200 to 1600 square feet.

One of the most common downsizer complaints about condo townhomes is the limited parking, as they usually have small driveways and single-car garages. As many Baby Boomers have two or more vehicles, as well as their Harley, this can be a major drawback.

Stacked Townhouses

While these often look like a multi-story condominium apartment building, stacked townhomes are typically built with two discrete living units above one another. Each suite may be either a single-floor or a two-story unit. As most stacked townhomes typically do not have elevators, they tend to be less appealing to downsizers and those with existing or progressive mobility challenges.

Condominium Apartment Suites

The most typical style of apartment condominiums are one-floor units ranging from 350-square-foot studio or bachelor suites (similar to a hotel room with a kitchenette) to expansive luxury penthouse multi-bedroom suites of 3000 square feet or more.

While some two-story units are available, often with windows spanning both floors, these units tend to "look better than they live" due to the limited floor space on each level and the amount of space lost to the staircase. Also, depending on their exposure, they can be very difficult to heat and cool due to the amount of glass, which tends to have a poor insulation factor.

> "WHETHER YOU ENJOY A GARDEN VIEW OR SKYLINE PERSPECTIVE, THERE IS A CONDOMINIUM PROPERTY THAT'S RIGHT FOR YOU."

Condominium apartment suites may be found in buildings ranging from three to more than 50 stories, with maintenance costs tending to be higher in low-rise buildings, as there are fewer units to share the common costs. As virtually all multi-level condominiums are equipped with elevators, they provide easier access for those with mobility challenges; however, unless specifically designated, downsizers should never assume that a suite is "handicap-enabled."

While the lobby, elevator, and front door to your condo apartment may accommodate devices such as walkers or wheelchairs, the doorways, interior hall, bathroom and galley-style kitchens are typically designed for optimal space utilization. It is recommended that accessible devices be tested inside any unit that you may be considering before becoming emotionally attached and choosing to buy the unit.

Typically, condo apartments are built with either a solarium or a balcony. The balcony may be quite spacious, but it is typically included in the floor space on which your monthly maintenance cost is based. Some buildings simply have a French or Juliette balcony, which is a patio door that opens to simulate the experience of a balcony.

When considering a condo apartment, it is important to understand that the costs associated with maintaining facilities such as an indoor swimming pool, fitness center, and multi-level underground parking garage, will increase as the complex ages.

> "Look for those amenities that you really want... You'll help pay for maintaining that pool whether you use it or not."

Newer "green" condo apartment buildings are promoted as being more energy-efficient, but the reality is that the costs of heat and electricity are the responsibility of each owner. On the surface, individually metered suites may appear to be a great idea, since you would not be paying for others who are less efficient in their use of utilities. However, one should remember that individual owners are paying "retail energy rates," whereas the condo complex may be able to buy gas and electricity at a more cost-effective bulk commercial rate. This cost would then be distributed over all units in the complex as part of their monthly maintenance fee, and may be lower than individual-usage billing.

WHERE IS THE RIGHT PLACE TO BUY YOUR DOWNSIZING CONDO?

One of the exciting aspects of buying an urban condominium is the amazing range of choices you have in terms of view, exposure, and the amenities nearby. These features are key considerations in most thoughtful condominium purchase decisions.

For those who love the romance of endless sunsets, a key criterion may be a western exposure. Others may want to watch the sunrise every day. Depending on your Downsizer Profile, the style and size of the suite chosen, and the building's orientation, you may even be able to have an unimpeded view of both.

Downtown

While the inner core of some major cities, such as New York, Los Angeles, Toronto and Montreal, are flourishing and transitioning into upscale lifestyle destinations, being downtown in other cities is less appealing. This is certainly a lifestyle of tradeoffs and contrasts, particularly for those moving from larger country or urban homes. But the lure of being at the heart of things and "closer to the action" can make it worthwhile.

> "While your choice of condo is a personal decision, don't forget that equity growth is inseparable from location, location, location."

As parking here is both limited and expensive, a car can be something of a liability. However, public transit is usually easily available and, in some cities, may run all night. Many downtown condo dwellers will simply rent a car when needed. Also, bicycles are experiencing a major resurgence among "downtowners" and, while this will not appeal to all Baby Boomers, it is a convenient and easy way to get around (as long as one is careful).

For those buyers looking to invest in residential rental properties, downtown condos on or near the subway are considered prime choices, as these are very popular with a large cross section of tenants who are able and willing to pay for quality rental suites with the right combination of amenities.

Waterfront

No matter where some people travel in the world, they are always drawn to the water, and condo dwellers are certainly no exception. Waterside properties typically offer good equity protection, bearing in mind, of course, that the more expensive units with optimal views will always appreciate in value more quickly and more consistently than those with a less appealing exposure. While access to public transit routes and shopping are important, many condo downsizers are willing to make a trade-off to be on or near the waterfront. This is especially true for those who enjoy an active outdoor lifestyle, with access to running, windsurfing, biking and other activities being a feature of the waterfront option.

Commuter Corridor

Many condominium townhomes and apartments are within a short walk of major subway, streetcar, or bus routes that make it easy to get virtually anywhere—often more quickly than by car during rush hour. These homes and suites offer excellent equity protection and resale potential, based on their appeal to a diverse audience of condo buyers. Downsizing investors looking for prime rental properties typically prioritize properties along major commuter corridors, which attract quality rental clients.

Suburban

Condominium complexes that are built in suburban communities tend to appeal to a different type of buyer. The land these are built on was often purchased at more attractive prices, making these generally more affordable. These units have also been built in response to market research indicating that many downsizers who live in the neighborhood wish to sell their family home and stay in the community, close to their friends and their traditional support services. Frequently several families will buy suites in a new complex at the same time in order to live close to one another.

OTHER CONSIDERATIONS WHEN CHOOSING A CONDOMINIUM COMMUNITY

Before finalizing your decision to purchase a specific unit or building, consider the following:

The offer to purchase should always be made conditional on your lawyer reviewing the status certificate, which includes information such as the adequacy of the reserve fund for current and future maintenance of the complex. It is also advisable to review the building bylaws with your lawyer to be sure you understand them, and that you are willing and able to adhere to these rules. In most condominium complexes, there are pet size and type restrictions that are strictly enforced. You will want to be sure that your dog Fifi is not on their "disallowed" list.

Ask your Real Estate & Downsizing Coach to take you for a tour of the parking garage. While previewing suites, observing the condition of the corridors and elevators in the complex will also give you valuable insights into the current condition and ongoing commitment to maintaining the building's common elements.

"YOUR REAL ESTATE & DOWNSIZING COACH WITH CONDO EXPERIENCE IS INVALUABLE WHEN CHOOSING THE RIGHT CONDO FOR YOUR LIFESTYLE AND BUDGET."

As you will be living in close proximity to many other residents who are sharing the same common spaces, thoughtful consideration of your compatibility with this environment will optimize your enjoyment and comfort in your new surroundings.

Although the excitement of moving into a fresh, personalized unit in a new condo building is exciting, you can expect some disruption during the first 6-to-18 months until the building, staff, and equipment settles down.

When deciding whether to buy a new or resale condo, remember that it may be more difficult to "get a feel" for the character and make-up of any condo complex until it has settled in.

7

BRINGING IT ALL BACK HOME

Having worked through the steps in this book, you are now ready to move to that final step that you have worked so hard to prepare for. Based on your personal Downsizing Profile, you and your partner have a much clearer picture of your "Next Chapter," including the style, type, budget, and general location of that ideal downsizing home for you.

Together with your Real Estate & Downsizing Coach, you are now ready to sell your home and ramp up your search for the property with the optimal combination of features you have prioritized.

CHOOSING THE RIGHT REAL ESTATE & DOWNSIZING COACH

Throughout this book, we have emphasized the importance of sound advice at each step of developing the Downsizing Plan that is specifically tailored to you and your partner's lifestyle needs. Although most downsizers assume that you sell your house and move first, you run the risk of choosing the destination before determining the lifestyle choices that are available to you.

By working with a qualified Real Estate & Downsizing Coach, as well as leveraging the unique tools and resources we have provided at www.TheBookonDownsizing.com you will be guided through the process of answering the "what, when, why now, with whom, and how much" questions first. Then, with your Downsizing Profile completed, your Downsizing Plan in hand, and a shared "Bucket List" that you and your partner are looking forward to experiencing together, you'll be ready to choose the perfect home that will become your "home base" through the "Next Chapter" of your lives.

> A QUALIFIED REAL ESTATE & DOWNSIZING COACH CAN HELP TO FACILITATE YOUR DOWNSIZING PLAN AND MAKE IT A REALITY."

Your Real Estate & Downsizing Coach is committed to your goals and assisting you in making the right decisions at each step of the process. Blessed with endless patience, insight, and good judgement, they will be a key resource on your downsizing team, ready to answer questions you may have along the way. For more information on connecting with the right Real Estate & Downsizing Coach in your area, go to www.TheBookonDownsizing.com.

MAKING IT HAPPEN: BUYING, SELLING, MOVING, AND GETTING SETTLED

The "Buy First or Sell First" Dilemma: Make the Decision That's Right for You

When the time is right to move ahead, this is always a challenging question. Obviously, you want to sell your home for as much as possible in order to maximize your return. If you are financially able to purchase your next home first, and then sell your current home, this is the best of all possible options, as you have secured the home you truly want and can now market your current home for all it's worth.

On the other hand, if you're unable to own two homes simultaneously, even for a short period of time, you may be tempted to search for that perfect home first and, should you find it, hope that the seller will accept a conditional offer dependent on you selling your current home quickly (typically within four to six weeks). However, they will continue to offer their home for sale and, in the event that they receive a firm offer, you may still lose that ideal home to another buyer.

Should this happen, it may feel like "the fish that got away" and you may start comparing every other home to that one. This can then start the spiral of the "4 Deadly Ds"—Disappointment, Discouragement, Dejection, and Demoralization. Robbed of your dream, you may even begin to regret starting the downsizing process.

> "ENJOY THE JOURNEY, BUT DON'T ALLOW YOURSELF TO MOVE IN EMOTIONALLY UNTIL THE DEAL IS DONE!"

At times like these, having a knowledgeable and sympathetic Real Estate & Downsizing Coach to guide you can be the difference between succumbing to despair and brushing off your disappointment and continuing to go forward. Armed with your Downsizing Plan and Profile, you'll be able to move ahead with getting your current home priced and promoted, and finding that other ideal home that is surely out there.

Preparing, Packaging, and Promoting the Sale of Your House

Having completed your plan and downsized the "stuff" you've chosen to let go, your home is now "minimalized" and "de-cluttered." It probably feels more spacious already and we are now ready to prep your home to be as bright and appealing as possible when prospective buyers come for a viewing.

Although promoting your home on the Internet and using social media broaden your reach, nothing takes the place of a realtor showing your home and explaining all of the features it has to offer. A personalized brochure that captures its essence and emotionally engages potential buyers with a room-by-room dialogue makes it easier for them to see their family already living there. And, finally, when a buyer submits an offer, your Real Estate & Downsizing Coach is there with you, ready not only to discuss the offer, but to support you as you review this last aspect of your old life and move on to that "Next Chapter."

The Search

Working with your Real Estate & Downsizing Coach makes buying the right downsizing home enjoyable and engaging. With the detailed analysis of what your "ideal home" will include, what your budget is, and where you prefer to be, the goal is now to find that special place.

While you were in the process of preparing your home for sale, your coach will have been researching the market for available homes that meet most, if not all, of your criteria. If the ideal home you have defined is not currently available, your coach may be able to identify similar homes that are not currently for sale and determine if any of these may be coming on the market soon.

> "YOUR DOWNSIZING PLAN CAN MAKE DISCOVERING YOUR 'NEXT CHAPTER' HOME AS THRILLING AS BUYING YOUR FIRST HOME."

It is truly an exciting experience visiting the type of homes that match your expressed preferences. As you walk through each home, you are assessing how it feels to you and your partner, while visually placing the furniture that you've chosen to bring with you. With a detailed plan and clearly defined objectives, the process of finding that right home can be an exhilarating experience.

When at last you find the home of your dreams, your coach will prepare a market assessment for this property so you can review comparable properties and decide what a reasonable offer would be. Your Real Estate & Downsizing Coach has been with you throughout this process, and now they will make sure that you receive the most favorable terms possible. In this way, there should be no surprises or disappointments on closing day, when you arrive at your new home with the keys.

If this process is going on simultaneously with your home being offered for sale, your coach will be able to communicate with you regularly and provide feedback from buyers who have viewed your home, as well as share any offers that may be pending. In this way, they are able to make everything as seamless as possible, while allowing you to enjoy *the thrill of the ride.*

Planning and Preparing in Advance Makes Packing and Moving Easy

Wow! It's hard to believe, but we are finally moving. And the best part is, it seems so easy.

You have already decided what you are taking with you, and most of the furniture and other "stuff" that is not going to your new home has already "disappeared." Packing is much easier, as the decisions about what to keep and where to store it have already been dealt with. We just pack the boxes, label them with the room for which they're designated, and the movers handle the rest.

On moving day, the garage or basement of your new home will not be crammed with boxes of things you don't know where to unpack. By the end of the day, virtually everything should be in its place and, with luck, those new furnishings and appliances you purchased have already been delivered, too.

5 STEPS TO GUARANTEE THAT YOU'LL LOVE LIVING IN YOUR NEW HOME IMMEDIATELY

Recognizing that, in most cases, *a house does not become a home* until you tailor it to your taste and your furnishings are in place, we recommend you take the following steps to ease the transition:

1. When possible, ask your Real Estate & Downsizing Coach to recommend a cleaning service, or to arrange on your behalf for the home to be thoroughly cleaned immediately upon closing, including washing all windows.

2. Meet with a décor consultant as soon as possible after you have purchased the home. Usually, you will be able to visit one or two times prior to closing for measuring purposes, and this is an ideal opportunity to get some professional input on how this home can be tailored to become *your envisioned downsizing home.*

> "HOME BUYERS FIND PROFESSIONALLY STAGED HOMES SO INVITING... WHAT IF YOUR 'NEXT CHAPTER' HOME WAS TOTALLY STAGED BEFORE YOU MOVED IN?"

3. Based on this consultation, ask for a quotation and, if practical, have these modifications completed, including any painting (both inside and outside) that may be required, as soon as possible. If you wait weeks or months to get to these tasks, the bloom of having finally arrived at the "Next Chapter" will lose some of its luster.

4. Ask your Real Estate & Downsizing Coach to recommend or arrange on your behalf for a landscaping service to take care of cutting the grass for the first month and, if required, ensure that the gardens and landscaping are kept in pristine condition. While you could probably do these chores yourself, it may be worth the cost to have this done for you until you can develop your new routines. Once you are settled, you can choose to continue with the service or assume these chores yourself.

5. Finally, you will want to host an Open House for friends and family to drop by and visit you on a specified day. With your home *beautifully dressed* and looking as you had imagined it, you will quickly realize that all of the thought and discussion that went into your Downsizing Plan was more than worth the effort. And, when your friends ask how you seem to have done it so easily, just smile and tell them, "it's all in the planning."

IN SUMMARY: WHY EMBRACING CHANGE NOW IS SO IMPORTANT

"LIFE HAPPENS, BUT IT'S NEVER TOO LATE TO FACE REALITY, ADAPT TO CHANGE, AND COMMIT TO LIVING DIFFERENTLY."

As noted earlier in the book, there is a percentage of middle-aged pre-retirees with no plan for their retirement. Their reasons or excuses vary, but the reality remains the same—if they do not act immediately to begin preparing for their future, they will be living at or near the edge. Though the lifestyle they are currently enjoying may be quite comfortable, without a realistic plan in place that takes account of anticipated changes in income and other variables, they will be unable to sustain their standard of living.

In her book *Never Too Late*, author Gail Vaz-Oxlade suggests pretending you and your partner just retired on a minimal fixed income. If there is no other income available to you, then, she suggests, you should immediately start downsizing your life—your possessions, your accommodations, and your spending—to live within this budget.

Impossible, you say? Well, if we do not act today, it will be thrust on us later. If you shrink your outflow now, you will be able to start saving money every month. And, if you have less than ideal health habits, by starting to eat the right foods and caring for your body, you may also be able to keep working longer and forestall the day when you have to retire.

Life is about choices and we should not allow the choice of how we spend our later years to be a matter of chance! Planning is the proactive decision to take responsibility for where each of us finds ourselves today. Then, without recriminations, we have to make hard choices about how and where we will spend our future. No one else can or will do this for us. It's our choice.

How a Downsizing Plan Can Overcome Resistance To Change

By understanding what downsizing is and developing a plan in conjunction with our partner, we can take away the fear, uncertainty, and doubt (FUD) that keeps us paralyzed and unwilling to consider change. While planning cannot identify unforeseen events that may occur, it can provide a defined process for dealing with these unanticipated challenges. It's this process of responding (based on our plan), rather than reacting to every incident, that allows us to deal with these challenges as they come up and minimize our stress and anxiety.

Setting realistic goals and timelines makes the process of downsizing fun, rewarding, and positive—changing negative stress (fear, anxiety, and a feeling of being out of control) into the "positive stress" associated with, for example, riding your first roller coaster. It's scary, but exhilarating!

The Importance of Teamwork

Trying to downsize alone or in a vacuum, with no outside input, can make the process much more daunting, if not impossible, for many of us. Even together with our partner, dealing with all of the emotions and micro-decisions necessary to keep the process moving smoothly can be a challenge. Hence the need for a support team, and the importance of picking your team carefully:

> "BY WORKING WITH POSITIVE TEAM MEMBERS WHO YOU RESPECT AND TRUST, YOU'LL MAINTAIN CONTROL AND AVOID FEELING OVERWHELMED."

- Choose people whom you respect rather than just like in order to give credence to their input.
- Choose people who are active and action-oriented. There is a job to be done and no amount of discussion will make it happen without action.
- Choose positive and upbeat people who can keep you laughing and having fun. When there are tears along the way, they will see you through it.

Just Do It

The best way to overcome inertia is simply to "get moving." Taking action sets the wheels in motion and it gets easier once there's forward momentum. As it's your plan and your "stuff," you need to take the lead. Your team can help, but decisions must be made constantly to keep the process going forward. If you delegate some of this decision-making responsibility, don't undermine the delegates by second-guessing their choices.

Be careful what you ask for. If you get frustrated and shout, "I don't care, just throw it in the bin," they probably will! Above all, remember that it is "the pot of gold at the end of the rainbow, not the rain before it" that is our objective in going through this downsizing process.

As stated earlier, it's choice, not chance that determines what happens to us in the future. To have the future we want, we need to make the personal choice that we deserve to have it, that we can only have it if we "let go" of our resistance to change, and that we must trust ourselves and the coaches we recruit to help us develop our Downsizing Plan in order to achieve it.

Choose to Downsize Before You Need To!

In our real estate practice, we regularly receive calls from older clients—or their distraught families—who find themselves suddenly confronted by the need to downsize their homes immediately, if not sooner. As we have discussed, "life happens" and we can suddenly be confronted with the necessity to act quickly, without the benefit of time, adequate discussion between spouses, or a defined plan. This can be especially traumatic when one partner or the family is faced with the task of sorting through a lifetime of "stuff," including nice furniture and collectibles, not to mention memorabilia, and finding no recipients who would appreciate receiving it.

> "AGING SENIORS WHO PROCRASTINATE IN MAKING DOWNSIZING-RELATED CHOICES UNFAIRLY SHIFT THIS BURDEN TO THEIR ALREADY STRETCHED FAMILY MEMBERS."

Whether the individual has passed, or now needs more care than can be provided in their current home, the result is a difficult transition, with unhappiness ebbing all around. In the latter case, the partner who has to leave the home may feel significant guilt for not having acted sooner. The other partner is typically overwhelmed and frustrated by their emotional and physical inability to cope with the task ahead, and the family has to put their own lives on hold to take on this additional responsibility.

In the end, the message is simply "when we fail to plan, we plan to fail." As a result, if we do not proactively develop our plan, however modest, enroll the help of our family or coaches as described in this book, and take action, then the result will be much more difficult than necessary.

The Freedom to Pursue
What's on Your "Bucket List"

One of the most exciting things in our lives was taking our first trip to Hong Kong and China, a major adventure that previously had seemed improbable, if not impossible, simply because we had never planned for it. On this journey, and on subsequent trips to Australia, India, West Africa, Turkey, Iceland, and Europe, we were able to realize our dreams of seeing the world, in ways we never thought possible.

We seldom meet a person who, when asked, cannot volunteer at least one thing they really wanted to do in their life, but never got to it. Life happened and time passed until the opportunity no longer seemed achievable or important. Don't let this happen to you!

> "YOUR JOURNEY OF A LIFETIME BEGINS WITH THE SEED OF AN IDEA, WATERED WITH COMMITMENT, AND MADE A REALITY WITH CAREFUL PLANNING."

Retirement and downsizing are two enablers that can free us to have the time, the resources, and the opportunity to pursue any dream we ever had. However, without planning, we risk letting time, health and mobility rob us of the chance to fulfill even one of these great adventures that life held for us.

If you still haven't taken the time to write out your "Bucket List," don't wait! Make a list of all the things that were once important for you to experience in your life. Next, prioritize the items on the list from 1 to 10 (10 being most important). Rewrite your "Bucket List" on a clean page starting with the most important first. Sign it at the bottom and date it. Now, on the back of that page, make a list of the things you would need to do so your #1 item could happen. Only by committing it to paper, signing it, and then writing down what needs to be done to make it so, will it ever happen.

As you think of other items that should be on the list, write them at the bottom of the page, and if they are really important, redo the list with these items in their proper place. To help you with this process, go to www.TheBookonDownsizing.com and complete your "Bucket List" profile.

Procrastination: Avoiding the Thief that Robs Your Future One Day at a Time

The word "procrastinate" is derived from the Latin word meaning "to put off until tomorrow." For some people, it seems to be a way of life, a means of indefinitely delaying dealing with things they'd rather avoid.

Planning to downsize is one of the most common things about which we procrastinate as we get older. "I just have too much stuff to get rid of," we say, while hoping that the mysterious entity that piled it up in their basement, and their garage, and their attic, and the $168 per month storage unit, will magically take it away too!

Every day that we put off doing the things we know inevitably must be done, we paralyze ourselves, while living with the underlying stress of this nagging thing that just won't go away.

One of the best antidotes to procrastination is to find a coach who can motivate us to start moving forward. All it takes is one small step, and then another, until the process of developing a Downsizing Plan develops its own momentum, as success builds on success.

The Key to Personal Happiness

Many of us have gone through life in pursuit of this thing called happiness, but when asked what it is, few can really explain it. The difficulty may lie in the fact that happiness isn't just one thing, but is really a "basket of feelings." This basket includes joy, contentment, peace of mind, and fulfillment. Although we cannot always determine if we are truly happy, we know if we feel inner joy or peace of mind, whether we are content, and when we feel fulfilled in what we do.

What does this have to do with downsizing? you may ask. The answer is that if we can determine what happiness is for us, we can then determine what gives us that deep inner sense of accomplishment in life. By separating this inner sense from the "stuff" that we normally associate with making us happy, the process of letting go gets much easier.

"OUR 'NEXT CHAPTER' IS SHAPED BY OUR CHOICES IN EMBRACING THE REALITIES OF AGING AND SHIFTING GEARS... GRACE AND HAPPINESS, OR RESISTING CHANGE TO THE END"

Seven Keys to Downsizing

Downsizing is a process, not an event

Downsizing encompasses more than your home

Downsizing is about "moving on" versus "hanging on"

Downsizing starts with simple planning

Downsizing is a team sport

Downsizing is an exciting journey

Downsizing requires action – just do it!

About the Authors

When Monika Lowry and her husband, Robert Miller, reflect on the life they've built together, they can't help but smile. Self-professed soul mates, it was a long and winding road to arrive here and, in their words, fulfill their destiny. Life threatening illnesses, cross-continent voyages, tireless hard work, Monika and Robert have faced enough adversity for two lifetimes and made some extremely difficult choices along the way. Still, both will tell you they consider themselves all the wiser – and stronger – for it.

An immigrant who saw more struggle than she'd care to recall before her seventh birthday, Monika still manages to be one of the most animated, positive individuals you'll ever encounter. She is also a successful business woman, passionate world traveller, and voracious reader with a zest for life that is nothing less than infectious. "I believe each day you have a choice to be happy and I willingly make that choice" she says.

Robert admires and shares his wife's outlook. After a health scare in 1991, he vowed to make the most of every day and never take anything for granted. A prolific and articulate writer, speaker and creative thinker, Robert has successfully blended his 40 years of face-to-face corporate and Real Estate client conversations with Monika's insights and wisdom to create "The Book on Downsizing".

CPSIA information can be obtained at www.ICGtesting.com
Printed in the USA
LVOW11*2047240815

451321LV00013B/949/P